Why Am I So MISERABLE?

If This is the Lord's Will

Anne Reynolds

LIBERTY
UNIVERSITY.
Press

Why Am I So Miserable If This is the Lord's Will
by Anne Reynolds

ISBN-13:   978-1-935986-06-5

All Scripture references taken from the New King James Version of the Bible, or where noted, from the New American Standard Version of the Bible.

MacArthur, John, ed. The MacArthur Study Bible. New King James Version. ©1997.

Zodhaites, Spiros, ed. The Hebrew-Greek Key Study Bible. New American Standard. Red letter edition. ©1990.

Reprinted by permission. "The new Strong's expanded dictionary of Bible words" c2001, Thomas Nelson Inc. Nashville, Tennessee. All rights reserved.

Reprinted by permission. "The vanishing conscience" MacArthur, John, 2005, Thomas Nelson Inc. Nashville, Tennessee. All rights reserved.

Websters New World Dictionary. Third College edition, Neufeldt, Victoria, and Guralink, David B., editors. Webster's New World Dictionaries, 1989. Reproduced with permission of John Wiley & Sons, Inc.

Simpson, A. B. Christ in you. Camp Hill, Pa.: Christian publications (used by permission, Christian and Missionary Alliance), c1997.

Subject headings:
Flesh and spirit antithesis (Pauline doctrine)
Sanctification
Christian life

Cover & Interior Design:

Megan Johnson
Johnson2Design
Johnson2Design.com

LIBERTY
UNIVERSITY.
Press
Lynchburg, VA

Contents

Introduction

ave you ever found yourself between a rock and a hard place? That is where I found myself not so long ago. It was 2002. Though that is now years ago, the experience I had then was so intense that I have not forgotten any of it; nor do I want to forget it.

The rock and hard place to which I refer is this: not being able to give up my faith on the one hand, and not being able to go on with it either. The crisis of faith came about when I started to feel that due to the circumstances I was in that being a Christian was pointless, joyless, and useless. I couldn't see how what I was doing was accomplishing anything. If you have ever felt that everything was futile, that there was no hope, and there was no joy and no blessing in your life, that is exactly how I felt. Every day was a struggle; tasks were accomplished merely through force of will, which was exhausting. So on top of being depressed and miserable, I became physically worn out. If this does not bring you to the end of your rope, I don't know what else will.

Complicating the whole situation is the spiritual struggle that went on. What I was experiencing at that time was not matching with the God I had experienced in the past. Despite how miserable I was, I knew that God was real and that my salvation was real. I had even experienced His comfort, help and strength in the past. There was no way I could turn my back on God or reject Christ, who I know paid the sacrifice for my sins.

This is what brought me to the "between a rock and a hard place." I could not tolerate my misery; neither could I possibly fathom the point to it. I could not see why God was allowing the pain I was in, or what could be the point of it. But I did know God and had experienced His love, so I couldn't abandon my faith either.

By God's grace I did find a solution to this dilemma. I thank the Lord for His patience with me! For though I could not feel His presence or see Him working in my life at the time of the trial I was in, He kept on working on me and in me. It is by His grace alone that I came through this trial; all that I now understand is only possible by His Spirit. But that is the end of the story; the questions yet to be answered are: How do you handle misery or suffering? How can this be part of God's will? What is God's will? How does the answer to these questions affect how we live the Christian life and our relationship with God and others?

"Being confident of this very thing, that he which hath begun a good work in you will perform it until the day of Jesus Christ"

—Philippians 1:6

"...this isn't the life I signed up for! I specifically remember signing up for great parents, a great marriage, and great kids... I signed up for lifelong friendships, thin thighs, and vibrant health. Instead, I find myself in the middle of a life I DIDN'T sign up for."[1]

Chapter 1
Being in the Will of God and Miserable?

*T*he will of God makes you miserable? How does that happen? How can the will of God result in misery? The two being in the same sentence just doesn't seem right or even possible. But whether it should be possible or not, I have experienced it. I can hear someone say: "Wait just a minute—are you sure that you are or were in the will of God?" and "You could only be miserable if you were not in the will of God."

Yet I am convinced that I was in the will of God and found myself in the most miserable state that I have ever been in. This being the case, it is important to explain what I considered the will of God for me was at that time, and how I came to that conclusion. The title of this book asks a question that assumes that I knew what the will of God was for my life. If I did not know, then I couldn't blame my misery on being in God's will. The question also makes a second assumption: that being in God's will should not result in misery.

That being said, how is the will of God determined, and how did I determine that I was in it? Many books have been written that discuss determining the will of God; what I propose to share here is a synopsis of what I believe the will of God is, and how I came to determine being in it.

What is the will of God? I base my definition on the Word of God. His will is expressed not only in direct statements of "The will of the Lord is…" but also in the commands He has given us. Jesus said that the greatest of the commandments was to love God and to love others, which was the sum of all the commandments (Matthew 22:37-40). Passages in which the will of God is mentioned describe both what He accomplishes and what He desires for us to do.

God's will is given in His Word as:

1. His determination, in which He either causes or prevents something from happening (what He does to fulfill His will); and

2. His desire, to see His children living according to His Word

Five examples of the Lord's will:

1. Our election: "Of His own will He brought us forth by the word of truth, that we might be a kind of firstfruits of His creatures." (James 1:18);

2. Our life and plans: "Instead you ought to say, 'If the Lord wills, we shall live and do this or that.'"(James 4:15);

3. His control over circumstances "I will return again to you, God willing" (Acts 18:21b);

4. Our resurrection and everlasting life: "And this is the will of Him who sent Me, that everyone who sees the Son and believes in Him may have everlasting life; and I will raise him up at the last day" (John 6:40);

5. Our predestination and adoption: "having predestined us to adoption as sons by Jesus Christ to Himself, according to the good pleasure of His will" (Ephesians 1:5).

The Lord's will is accomplished when we:

1. Give thanks in everything (1 Thessalonians 5:18);

2. Abstain from sexual immorality (1 Thessalonians 4:3);

3. Do not live according to the lusts of the flesh (1 Peter 4:2);

4. Do good: "For this is the will of God, that by doing good you may put to silence the ignorance of foolish men" (I Peter 2:15); and

5. Do not love the world (I John 2:15-17).

God gave us His Word so that we would have guidelines for determining His will. Even if we cannot find chapter and verse stating specifically where we should live, or what career we should pursue, there are principles that we can follow in Scripture. Examples of these principles are:

1. I Corinthians 10:31 "...do all to the glory of God;"

2. "the steps of a man are established by the Lord" (Psalm 37:23, NASB) (God makes the way possible; He opens and closes doors of opportunity);

3. To not be unequally yoked (2 Corinthians 6:14);

4. The use of spiritual gifts, as detailed in 1 Corinthians 12;

5. To marry or remain single? The Apostle Paul gives guidelines for singles in 1 Corinthians 7; and

6. How to select a future husband or wife? Qualities, such as love and submission, to be looked for are given in Ephesians. 6: 22-31 and Colossians. 3:18-19.

But what if we cannot find a principle that addresses the question or situation specifically? How do we know when we are making the right decision? How do we know we are in the right job or place, or marrying the right person? What if we have used all the standards of Scripture (not being unequally yoked and so forth) and still are not sure?

In situations like those, Scripture does guide us as well, with admonition to pray always (1 Thessalonians 5:17) and to wait on the Lord (Psalm 27:14). A good principle to keep in mind is that if unsure, wait until the Lord makes the way clear. We do not serve a God who plays some sort of guessing game with us. Search the Scriptures regarding whatever situation for any principles or precepts that can be applied and that we may be unaware of. When dealing with situations that are not directly addressed in Scripture, (i.e. what house to purchase) indirect principles such as being wise and prudent (Proverbs) apply. God also will reveal His will by His control over circumstances. This has often been referred to as opened and closed doors.

It is important, however, not to read the Lord's will into every event that happens. An example of this happened to me when going to a job interview. I was seated next to a missionary on the plane who lived near my potential place of employment. She offered to help me find a place to live. It would be easy to think, "This job must be God's will!" That would only be the case if I actually get the job as a result of the interview—I didn't!

Determining the Lord's will, when it is not something expressly stated in Scripture, is something we cannot not be dogmatic about. If we have not married yet; if we are married but have no children; or if there seems to be a lack of God's blessing in our life, people tend to judge where only God is qualified to make the judgment. "You're not married? What's wrong with you? Did you miss an opportunity, have you missed God's plan for your life?" I have been asked these questions by well-meaning people. But any such question implies that God is impotent in some way and is dependent on us to figure out what His will is before it can be accomplished. God is omnipotent. "I am Almighty God" (Genesis 17:1). If there are any limits to God's power, they are only what God Himself has placed there. If God wants us to do something, He makes it clear in His Word what He expects us to do. We also have the indwelling Holy Spirit that convicts of sin and alerts us to error. If we are not disobeying the Word of God or violating our conscience, then we have not missed the will of God, regardless of our circumstances.

God is always consistent with His Word. Experience or feelings can lead us astray. Both experience and emotion cannot be relied upon because our experience can only be viewed from a fallible, limited human perspective; emotions are not rational and should never be relied upon for a decision. The only truly consistent and reliable guidance comes from God and His Word.

In addition to praying and waiting on the Lord, one of the guidelines that we can use in determining God's will is found in both the Old and New Testaments. Proverbs 20:18 states: "Plans are established by counsel." Seeking Godly counsel and advice from other believers is to decide things in a God-honoring way. 2 Corinthians 13:1 (NASB) states: "Every fact is to be confirmed by the testimony of two or three witnesses." This quote was referring to the instruction given in Deuteronomy 19:15. I realize that the context in Deuteronomy is dealing with a legal matter; but whether it is a legal matter or not, this principle can be seen in action when other believers confirm a course of action or vocation in our lives. In regard to both my occupation and my vocation (spiritual gift) I have had at least two witnesses tell me (unprompted) that I was doing or pursuing what they believed I was gifted in and should be doing.

God also reveals His will to us through His Spirit. Jeremiah tried to keep silent when the Lord had given him a message to speak but couldn't. "Then I said, 'I will not make mention of Him, nor speak anymore His name.' But His word was in my heart like a burning fire shut up in my bones; I was weary of holding it back, and I could not" (Jeremiah 20:9). If God wants us to do something, He will make it clear to us, and He will enable us to do it. (We will be miserable if we don't do it). This is evidenced by the fact that God is the truth (John 14:6), it is Satan that is the liar and deceiver (John 8:44;

Revelation12:9), and from the many examples of when God wanted someone to do something, He told them. We also know that "He who has begun a good work in you will complete it" (Philippians 1:6).

Based on what Scripture reveals about seeking Godly counsel, having a matter confirmed by two witnesses, and the providence of God in opening and closing doors, I believed that I was in the will of God. I was also seeking to live in obedience to His Word. I knew that I could not be where I was had God not opened the way; I also had more than one person tell me that I ought to be doing what I should be doing. This addresses the first issue, now what of the second?

The second issue or question to be answered is, doesn't being in the will of God mean being blessed? How can suffering (physically or emotionally) be part of His will? This is the crux of the problem that I was facing.

My dilemma was due in part to the fact that as a Christian I attended church, sang in the choir, taught Sunday School, helped with church suppers, and decorated bulletin boards; perhaps involved more than most, not as much as others. I had what I thought was a good relationship with God. I had daily devotions; Bible study also was a regular part of my life. When I prayed, I didn't just list my requests; I shared my heart with God.

Although I struggled with sin and the flesh, I always repented and sought to do God's will. By the time I was in my 30s, I thought I understood what I needed to understand in order to become spiritually mature. Well, I would not be writing all this if I did not have a great deal yet to learn; in fact, I discovered that my whole approach to living the Christian life was wrong. This can be unsettling to say the least. When you have been living your life a certain way for 20 odd years thinking it was the right way when it was not, it is both discouraging and devastating. It isn't just a matter of pride that made me reluctant to accept this kind of error; it was that so much of what I had done in the past had been done for the wrong reasons, and therefore a good deal of what I thought had value amounted to nothing. My thinking was that a life lived fairly well was not. I was faced with a choice: either I throw in the towel and forget the whole business, or stop doing what is wrong, and start doing what is right (repent). But I am getting ahead of myself.

First, just where did I go wrong? I had been taught to do good, and God will bless you. Do evil and you will not be blessed, but cursed (Deuteronomy 7:9-10). Since I wanted to honor God and be blessed, I sought to do the right things. Even though I had been careful to follow all the rules, I found myself in a miserable state, which I blamed on circumstances. I realized at the time that my circumstances were not the worst that I could have experienced. But for me what it amounted to was: no ministry, no church, no friends, no husband, and a different culture. Part of the reason for this was that I had moved from one state to another and was separated from family and friends. But included in this was that the church I was moving away from was splitting apart. There had been problems there which myself, my family and others had approached Biblically; unfortunately, the person in sin did not repent. Not only that, but there were others in the church who chose to believe the offender, rather than believing those offended, whom they had known for decades. By God's grace, I was able to forgive the offender, as well as those who did not support us. I prayed for all of them. But in moving away, it was with the knowledge that the church I once knew no longer existed. Losing that church was like losing a home. I had had a teaching ministry there, and I was very burdened for the women who still remained there In losing that church, my hopes for what it could become were lost as well In all, with the combination of grief over loss of my home church, I wasn't finding a church in my new location, and, therefore, had trouble finding friends outside of work.

I could not understand. I was sure I was where I was supposed to be, doing what I was supposed to be doing. I was sure the Lord wouldn't have led me where it didn't include a new ministry in a local church, among other things. In fact, all of the doors where I had been had closed one by one, and I interpreted that to mean that the Lord wanted me to get involved in ministry elsewhere. I would not have made the move if I had not prayed over and given the decision a great deal of consideration. I went, filled with peace and contentment, as well as excitement with what the Lord was going to do.

Surprise! What I thought I would find there wasn't there. Initially, I was patient. I thought, "Well it is just going to take time"—only the things I expected (friends, a church family) never materialized. The churches I found were either too liberal in their theology or too legalistic for me to join in good conscience. Though I found places to attend, a teaching ministry never developed. I was puzzled to say the least. In the first couple of months, it was simply discouraging; and it did not take long before I was depressed. I am not talking about the blues here. I was in a deep, dark pit emotionally. I felt betrayed. I cannot remember ever being so low in my whole life. How could I be in so much pain when I had always tried to do the right thing? Was God punishing me? Had I done something wrong?

No matter how much I studied, analyzed, and prayed about it, I couldn't figure it out. As far as I could tell, I hadn't done anything wrong; if I hadn't done anything wrong, why was I in the situation I was in? I believed, and do believe now, that God is in control, and that if He wanted something to change, that He would do it. But He didn't change anything. He did not change my circumstances or remove me from them in some way.

For me, the solution that seemed the most sensible and logical was for my circumstances to change from difficult and painful to easy and enjoyable. Didn't blessing mean good circumstances? If I was supposed to be blessed for doing the right things, then why didn't God provide them?

I thought perhaps it was just a matter of timing. God was going to bless me, but just not yet. It wasn't the right time. So I waited. After five months, I had reached the end of my rope. I reached a crisis point of faith. I was in so much emotional pain that I could hardly see straight; I thought that if this

Why Am I So Miserable If This is the Lord's Will

is what is meant by the blessings found in Christ, who wants it? As much as I couldn't see the point in continuing on, I couldn't give up my faith, for I had experienced God; I had come to know His love, comfort and grace throughout my Christian walk. I was stuck between a rock and hard place. What usual comforts I found through reading, eating or watching TV were of no use altogether.

The solution came only by God's grace. John Piper, in his book *Future Grace*, notes that:

"Since sin always brings misery, and misery is always experienced by sinners, therefore all of God's acts of grace are also acts of mercy, and all of his acts of mercy are also acts of grace. Every act of grace shown to a person because he is a sinner is also an act of mercy because his sin brings misery." [2]

It was totally by God's grace and mercy to me a sinner that it was revealed to me the cause of my misery (sin) and its remedy (repentance). My mother gave me *Shattered Dreams* by Larry Crabb to read. I was reluctant to read it. I was familiar with his writings and wasn't in the mood for further analysis. But when I reached the end of my rope, I thought, why not? It couldn't hurt anything. I was surprised when I started reading his book; it wasn't so much psychological in nature as it was spiritual. I won't go into detail about the book, but I recommend it. Out of everything he wrote in that book, one thing in particular stuck in my brain: Christ is better. God wouldn't let me forget it. I knew that it was true; I just did not know how to believe it. How could Jesus be better than what I wanted? As I write that sentence now, the question seems ridiculous. Christ is so much better there is no comparison. But at the time, I was so miserable I could not see it. I thought I knew Christ, that I loved Him. How was what I had with Him better, when the lack of what

I thought I needed and wanted was causing so much pain? Even if I could not understand it, I knew it was true. For the first time, I prayed correctly: I confessed my lack of faith, and prayed that He would increase it.

It is important to note here that God did not answer that prayer right away. I prayed for two weeks before God answered my prayer. This I want to make clear: the faith with which I believed was totally God's gift. I did not come to understand by any mental ability. Neither was it due to an emotional experience. I did not feel anything until God enabled me to believe. It was the understanding and belief that I was given that resulted in an emotional response. I was not able to receive this gift until I had come to an end of myself, until I had completely and utterly laid myself at His feet. This I know: you cannot be filled with the presence of God if you are full of yourself.

God's answer is very hard to describe. He did not speak to me in so many words. It was a combination of a sudden understanding and subsequent belief with an overwhelming sense of His presence. I sat there stunned for some time afterward. It was as if God was saying to me, "You do not think Christ is better? What do you think now?" Not that my situation was anything like Job's, but like Job I wanted to say: "Behold, I am vile; what shall I answer You? I lay my hand over my mouth" (Job 40:4).

Although I did develop some friendships over the next two years, my circumstances did not change. But by God's grace, I did! Praise God. Since that time, knowing Him has been the priority in my life. My passion is to die to self, to walk in the Spirit. It is not to live for what I want, but for what He wants.

God enabled me to believe, and showed me how much Christ is better. He also showed me that circumstances do not make us miserable; we make ourselves miserable when we don't seek God or consider God above everything else. This answers the question that is the title of the book. We can be in God's will, in the sense that we are where He wants us to be, doing what we should be doing, and can be miserable at the same time if we are not finding in Him what we need. Being in God's will was not what was making me miserable; it was looking for satisfaction and blessing in my circumstances, rather than in my relationship with God. Through this experience, I realized what my sin was: instead of focusing on the Giver (God) I was focusing on the gift (blessings). Instead of serving God, I was serving the flesh or my emotions. I considered pain my enemy, not sin (which separates me from God). Knowing God, knowing Jesus is the blessing, not what He gives; knowing Him is infinitely better than any immediate gratification that this world provides or that our flesh craves.

How I wish that what one comes to understand will be automatically applied and lived! As long as I live, or any of us live, there will always be the struggle with the flesh. What comes automatically is what comes naturally: walking according to the flesh. As we deal with each sin, each failing, and strive to live and walk in the Spirit, we will develop godly habits; there will be more successes in Christ than failures. Walking in the Spirit is only possible by the Spirit. It requires submission, dependence, repentance, grace, faith, trust, and obedience.

One last comment: while it is very true that sin is to be despised, I have learned that what is worse than sinning is not being willing to admit to it:

"If we say that we have no sin, we deceive ourselves, and the truth is not in us. If we confess our sins, He is faithful and just to forgive us our sins and to cleanse us from all unrighteousness. If we say that we have not sinned, we make Him a liar, and His word is not in us."
—1 John 1:8-10

It is much easier to think we are alright, that although we're "not perfect" there isn't really any need for revival in our life; after all, we have a relationship with God, and are actively serving Him. We repented at salvation; we have been following the "rules" and living a life of good repute. What is there to repent of? Plenty!

While it is true that we are washed by the blood of the Lamb, we are still sinners saved by grace; the price for our sin has been paid, but the flesh was not removed. The flesh is ever present with us and we cannot ever forget that. We can never think that we are okay, but must be ever diligent, on guard against the flesh. As we mature in Christ, there will be an ever-increasing awareness of our sinfulness and a desire to be holy as He is holy (1 Peter 1:13-16). "But of Him you are in Christ Jesus, who became for us wisdom from God—and righteousness and sanctification and redemption—that, as it is written, *'He who glories, let him glory in the LORD.'* "(1 Corinthians 1:30-31)

> *"Apart from thee I quickly die,*
>
> *bereft of thee I starve,*
>
> *far from thee I thirst and droop;*
>
> *but thou art all I need.*
>
> *Let me continually grasp the promise,*
>
> *I will never leave thee nor forsake thee."* 3

The crisis point in my spiritual journey several years ago was a turning point for me. Once I realized that I was trying to work out my own sanctification according to fleshly strategies and strength, and not by submission to the Spirit of God, I wanted to begin anew. I sought to understand through God's Word how sanctification is accomplished, and what the struggle with the flesh was all about. This being said, just how are we sanctified?

For we are His workmanship, created in Christ Jesus for good works, which God prepared beforehand that we should walk in them.

– Ephesians 2:10

"The ultimate goal of the church is not evangelism, important and indispensable as that ministry is. The ultimate goal is stated by Paul when he wrote: 'We proclaim him, teaching everyone with all wisdom, *so that we may present everyone perfect [mature] in Christ'*"

– Colossians 1:28 [4]

Chapter 2
Sanctification

*S*anctification is simply the process in the Christian life by which we are made holy, conformed to the image of Christ. "But we all, with unveiled face beholding as in a mirror the glory of the Lord, are being transformed into the same image from glory to glory, just as by the Spirit of the Lord." (2 Corinthians 3:18)

How does sanctification take place? (What is the process?) Do we accomplish our own sanctification? Do we play any part in it? Given below is an example of how the sanctification process is seen in many believers' lives, and previously in my own:

Salvation →Thankful for free gift → Strive to obtain more
gifts and blessings

=

Living for what God gives you;

believing life is all about you.

If our Christian walk is based on this formula, we do only what we think is required for more gifts or blessings and are puzzled when we do what we think is required and then don't receive them. This presents us with a choice: to get the gifts we want through our own efforts and fleshly means, or to reevaluate our whole approach to how the Christian life is lived and start walking by faith, according to the Spirit.

If we choose to reevaluate our approach to living the Christian life so that it is not about having what we want, the sanctification process then looks like this:

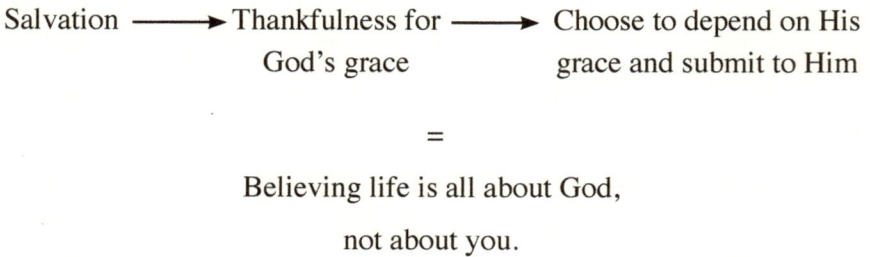

Salvation ——→ Thankfulness for ——→ Choose to depend on His
                    God's grace   grace and submit to Him

=

Believing life is all about God,

not about you.

If our Christian walk is based on this formula, we will discover that the best "gift" is God Himself; that a life lived seeking gifts rather than the Giver is a vain pursuit. To live our Christian life according to the first formula is to not be sanctified at all. For to be made holy, like Christ, is to not be self-centered, but God-centered. ("Love ... does not seek its own," 1 Corinthians 13:4-5)

Jesus did not die just to pay the penalty for sin, but to set us free from the bondage of sin, to be free from the pursuit of the pleasures of the flesh. What Jesus has accomplished for us:

1. Paid the penalty for our sin, provided salvation and eternal life

"He who has the Son has life; he who does not have the Son of God does not have life" (1 John 5:12). "For God so loved the world that He gave His only begotten Son, that whoever believes in Him should not perish but have everlasting life" (John 3:16). "For the wages of sin is death, but the gift of God is eternal life in Christ Jesus our Lord" (Romans 6:23). "But we see Jesus, who was made a little lower than the angels, for the suffering of death crowned with glory and honor, that He, by the grace of God, might taste death for everyone. For it was fitting for Him, for whom are all things and by whom are all things, in bringing many sons to glory, to make the captain of their salvation perfect through sufferings" (Hebrews 2:9-10). "But of Him you are in Christ Jesus, who became for us wisdom from God—and righteousness and sanctification and redemption ..." (1 Corinthians 1:30).

2. Our sanctification

"For both He who sanctifies and those who are being sanctified are all of one, for which reason He is not ashamed to call them brethren... Inasmuch then as the children have partaken of flesh and blood, He Himself likewise shared in the same, that through death He might destroy him who had the power of death, that is, the devil, and release those who through fear of death were all their lifetime subject to bondage. For indeed He does not give aid to angels, but He does give aid to the seed of Abraham. Therefore, in all things He had to be made like His brethren, that He might be a merciful and faithful High Priest in things pertaining to God, to make propitiation for the sins of the people. For in that He Himself has suffered, being tempted, He is able to aid those who are tempted" (Hebrews 2:11, 14-18). "But now having been set free from sin, and having become slaves of God, you have your fruit to holiness, and the end, everlasting life." (Romans 6:22) "But of Him you are in Christ Jesus, who became for us wisdom from God—and righteousness and sanctification and redemption..." (1 Corinthians 1:30).

3. Opportunity for fellowship with God and each other

For both He who sanctifies and those who are being sanctified are all of one, for which reason He is not ashamed to call them brethren, saying: 'I will declare Your name to My brethren; in the midst of the assembly I will sing praise to You.' And again: 'I will put My trust in Him.' And again: 'here am I and the children whom God has given Me'" (Hebrews 2:11-13). "Abide in Me, and I in you. As the branch cannot bear fruit of itself, unless it abides in the vine, neither can you, unless you abide in Me" (John 15:4). "That which we have seen and heard we declare to you, that you also may have fellowship with us; and truly our fellowship *is* with the Father and with His Son Jesus Christ. And these things we write to you that your joy may be full" (1 John 1:3-4).

He died that we might live for Him, according to His Spirit; He did not die that we might live comfortably in our flesh, living our lives according to our fleshly desires. "What shall we say then? Shall we continue in sin, that grace may abound? Certainly not! How shall we who died to sin live any longer in it? Or do you not know that all of us who have been baptized into Christ Jesus have been baptized into His death?" (Romans 6:1-3) To be His disciple means to "take up your cross and follow me" (Mark 10:21). It is giving up our will, way, and living according to His will, His way, and His desire. There is no middle ground.

Not only did Jesus provide salvation, but He also is the one who sanctifies us. We do not accomplish our sanctification; it is Jesus who sanctifies us. Why is this important? It means that I cannot reform my flesh; the flesh can only be denied. "For if you will live according to flesh you will die; but if by the Spirit you put to death the deeds of the body, you will live" (Romans 8:13). It also means that I cannot accomplish sanctification in others. What

I know will not change anyone's life. It is what God reveals to them from His Word and His Spirit as they obey His Word that will change their life. Pastors, teachers, churches cannot accomplish sanctification. Only Jesus accomplishes our sanctification.

What part, then, do we play in it, if any at all? If Jesus does the work, we need to let Him do it, and cooperate with Him either in obedience, repentance, submission and dependence on Him. What about pastors, teachers, churches? Their purpose is to feed the flock. Jesus said to Peter, "Feed my sheep" (John 21:17). This is the most important ministry that a pastor or teacher can do: to present the will of God as revealed in His Word. As God does not force His will on us, it is our choice and responsibility to submit to the work of sanctification that Jesus Christ accomplishes.

Not only are teaching and preaching the Word essential, encouragement and compassion for each believer is also essential. It is easy for a believer to become too comfortable, not even being aware that they are not living according to the will of God. They need loving encouragement to take a fresh look at their Christian walk by encountering God through His Word and prayer. Compassion is needed, for we only see the outward; God sees the heart. There will be those who don't appear to respond as we think they should; we need to pray for them and depend on God to work in them.

How is sanctification manifested in a believer's life? How is fleshly behavior distinguished from what is spiritual? Are there stages of growth? If so, how are they described? In answer to the first question, sanctification is manifested by any behavior that reflects the fruit of the Spirit. Galatians 5:19-24 not only describes this fruit, it distinguishes between that which is of the flesh and that which is of the Spirit:

"Now the works of the flesh are evident, which are: adultery, fornication, uncleanness, lewdness, idolatry, sorcery, hatred,

contentions, jealousies, outbursts of wrath, selfish ambitions, dissensions, heresies, envy, murders, drunkenness, revelries, and the like...But the fruit of the Spirit is love, joy, peace, longsuffering, kindness, goodness, faithfulness, gentleness, self-control. Against such there is no law. And those who are Christ's have crucified the flesh with its passions and desires."

The only way to have the fruit of the Spirit is to walk in the Spirit (Galatians 5:16). It is continually being dependent on, having conversation with, and being in submission to the Spirit, Son, and Father. In the same chapter, verse 18, those who walk in the Spirit are also described as being led by the Spirit. We cannot be led unless we are willing to follow. When Jesus called his disciples, He invited them to follow Him. He also said that for those that are weary and heavy-laden, to "take My yoke upon you and learn from Me... for My yoke is easy and My burden is light" (Matthew 11:29-30). We are also commanded to love God (Matthew 22:37), God calls us to follow Him, love Him, and surrender our will for His.

In answer to "Are there stages of growth?," yes. The degree in which we incorporate God in our lives—the more we love Him, trust Him, and obey Him—becomes the true indicator of our level of spiritual maturity.

What does God's Word say about spiritual growth or maturity?

1. We grow through the Word of God: " ... as newborn babes, desire the pure milk of the word, that you may grow thereby" (1 Peter 2:2)

2. Spiritual babes can only receive the milk of the Word and not meat: "And I, brethren, could not speak to you as to spiritual people but as to carnal, as to babes in Christ. I fed you with milk and not with solid food; for until now you were not able to receive it, and even now you are still not able; for you are still carnal" (1 Corinthians 3:1-3a)

3. Spiritual babes are characterized by carnal (fleshly) behavior (1 Corinthians 3:1-3)

4. Those who are mature press on toward the goal for the prize of the upward call in Christ Jesus. "Not that I have already attained, or am already perfected; but I press on, that I may lay hold of that for which Christ Jesus has also laid hold of me. Brethren, I do not count myself to have apprehended; but one thing I do, forgetting those things which are behind and reaching forward to those things which are ahead, I press toward the goal for the prize of the upward call of God in Christ Jesus. Therefore let us, as many as are mature, have this mind; and if in anything you think otherwise, God will reveal even this to you." (Philippians 3:12-15).

5. Those who are spiritual (mature) restore those who are fallen: "Brethren, if a man is overtaken in any trespass, you who are spiritual restore such a one in a spirit of gentleness, considering yourself lest you also be tempted" (Galatians 6:1).

6. Those who are mature teach the Word, those who are immature still need to be taught: "For though by this time you ought to be teachers, you need someone to teach you again the first principles of the oracles of God; and you have come to need milk and not solid food" (Hebrews 5:12).

If we are characterized by fleshly behavior more than Christ-like behavior; if we still have not gotten a handle on the "first principles" and need to be taught, we are still spiritual babes in Christ. Those who are spiritually mature will manifest Christ-like behavior; they will teach others and restore the fallen. They will walk in the Spirit and not according to the flesh. Spiritual maturity takes place as we submit to the Spirit and deny the flesh. The more we give into the flesh and serve it, the more we distance ourselves from God;

spiritual growth and maturity cannot take place. Spiritual health and vitality, then, are determined by our relationship with God; how we relate to Him. When we strive after God, we strive for righteousness.

Characteristics of spiritual maturity (walking in the Spirit) are the qualifications given in 1 Timothy 3:2-9 for both pastor and deacon:

> *"A bishop then must be blameless, the husband of one wife, temperate, sober-minded, of good behavior, hospitable, able to teach; not given to wine, not violent, not greedy for money, but gentle, not quarrelsome, not covetous; one who rules his own house well, having his children in submission with all reverence (for if a man does not know how to rule his own house, how will he take care of the church of God?); not a novice, lest being puffed up with pride he fall into the same condemnation as the devil. Moreover he must have a good testimony among those who are outside, lest he fall into reproach and the snare of the devil. Likewise deacons must be reverent, not double-tongued, not given to much wine, not greedy for money, holding the mystery of the faith with a pure conscience."*

From this it can be seen that those in ministry, whether they are Pastor, elder, or deacon, need to demonstrate a life that is in submission to God and to His Spirit. Fleshly characteristics (drunkenness, violence, greed) will not define them, but the fruit of the Spirit will (temperance, hospitality, gentleness). Other characteristics that apply to anyone in leadership: a pure conscience, discipline in the home, a good testimony, and not being double-tongued (talking out of both sides of your mouth!). All of these are a result of a love for God and daily repentance and sensitivity to sin.

A godly man or woman is not defined by whether they have sinned or not; they are defined by an acute awareness of their sin and sinfulness and desire

Why Am I So Miserable If This is the Lord's Will

to be rid of it and restored to fellowship with God and others. Repentance of sin at salvation makes a relationship with God possible; continual repentance sustains it. "Life in the Spirit is not life without sin; it is life spent learning to hate sin, to love God, and to yearn with an ever-increasing passion for the time when God's goodness will reign in our hearts forever."[5*]

Repentance called for after salvation is recorded in Revelation 2:5, when the church at Ephesus is urged to repent and renew its fellowship with Christ. Sin is the enemy, because it keeps us from experiencing God. Being in fellowship with God means walking according to His way by His enabling; as we submit to His will, we are sanctified by the work of Jesus Christ.

This 'sanctification' process is the primary means by which we come to know whether or not we have saving faith, and it continues throughout the lives of true believers. We do not earn our salvation through the process, but it is God's way of showing us that we truly belong to Him, that we have a heart of faith. And we must be very clear: having a heart of faith is not the same as being without sin.[6]*

When a spiritually mature person sins, their intolerance for sin will be shown in their willingness to confess their sin and repent of it as quickly as possible.

Churches fail, not only because of the lack of good leadership, but because the congregation is not pursuing a right relationship with the Lord. Faith in a program, in a person, or in rules or traditions, fails to put faith in the Lord. Many Christians think they have a good relationship with the Lord, simply because they faithfully attend church, teach Sunday School, sing in the choir, etc. Unfortunately, cults do the same thing. Doing all these things does not save us; neither does it mean that we are walking in the Spirit. Unless we

---

* Righteous sinners: the believer's struggle with faith grace, and works; Julian Ron. c1998. Used by Permission of NavPress, All Rights Reserved. www.navpress.com (1-800-366-7788).

choose to include God in our life and in the decisions that we make, we will live life on our terms, independent from the Lord.

Independent action apart from God is always sin. Eve sinned because she chose to do things on her terms—Adam likewise. Independent action indicates an attitude that says we either disagree with what God has provided or said, or that we do not need God. It says: "I can do this myself," "I want to do this my way," "God isn't providing for me what I need," "I must protect myself" (God doesn't seem to be doing it), and "I just want to have some fun" (it won't hurt anything). All such statements are wrong. We always need God, and not just when we are in trouble. God may not give us what we want, but He'll always take care of us; God may not keep us from trials, and from getting hurt, but He will get us through — with love, comfort, peace, and strength, enabling us to come through it rejoicing if we trust and depend on Him. Knowing this, anything that is going to come between God and us, including fun, should be considered as the extra weight that we toss aside as we run the race (Hebrews 12:1). As we come to know and love Him more, this becomes our desire, for there is nothing that compares with Him.

The goal for all Christians is spiritual maturity. We can all have a good relationship with God. It isn't enough to read the Word of God or hear it; we must experience it as we live in obedience to it. To follow instruction from His Word without understanding that only God makes it possible to do so will only result in trying to live the Christian life in our own (fleshly) strength, which always fails. As we obey and trust God while depending on Him, our love will grow for Him; and as we obey and trust Him, we experience a relationship with Him that is not possible otherwise. We need never think that only a person in leadership is capable of honoring God on "that level" or that we will never know God or experience God like they do. Spiritual maturity is possible for every believer, because God makes it possible. Those who do not progress in the spiritual walk with God do so because of disobedience. God loves us and wants our sanctification, which is for our good.

Why Am I So Miserable If This is the Lord's Will

To believe that Jesus Christ is better than anything else that we could ever want requires faith. Walking in the Spirit is a walk of faith every day, for our flesh is always in opposition to the Spirit (Galatians 5:17). We are continually presented with the choice to either believe that what our flesh wants is what we need and have to have, or that God and His way are better. The nature of our relationship with God, then, is defined by what we choose: to follow Him or our flesh. Good works are only valid if they are done in service to God and not for appearance's sake. Faith does produce works, but there are works without faith. We believe that salvation is by grace through faith (Ephesians 2:8-9), and then proceed to live the Christian life in the flesh by not seeking to depend on the grace of God but depending on ourselves instead. "Are you so foolish? Having begun in the Spirit, are you now being made perfect by the flesh?" (Galatians 3:3). How can works of the flesh ever please God? (They won't). The difference between walking in the flesh and walking in the Spirit is not only what we are doing, it is why and how we are doing what we are doing.

Why and how we do what we do—this indicates whether we are acting in submission to the Lord or pleasing ourselves or others. Why do we have both a desire to please God and to please ourselves? Scripture gives us the answer: the fleshy, sinful nature we inherited through Adam.

O God of the highest heaven,

Occupy the throne of my heart,

Take full possession and reign supreme,

Lay low every rebel lust,

Let no vile passion resist thy holy war;

Manifest thy mighty power,

And make me thine for ever.[7]

"For those who live according to the flesh set their minds on the things of the flesh, but those who live according to the Spirit, the things of the Spirit. For to be carnally minded is death, but to be spiritually minded is life and peace. Because the carnal mind is enmity with God; for it is not subject to the law of God, nor indeed can be. So then, those who are in the flesh cannot please God."

– Romans 8:5-8

Chapter 3
Our Flesh

What does it mean to walk in the Spirit and not according to the flesh? The way I was living the Christian life was not working because I was trying to live the Christian life in the strength of my flesh rather than through the strength that only the Holy Sprit can provide. What God had revealed to me up to this point was that I was attempting to live the Christian life to benefit my flesh, avoiding pain, and trying to get what I wanted and please God at the same time. This approach failed and will always fail; to live life according to such a philosophy (whether we are conscious of it or not) only puts us into bondage.

It was and is my desire now to not walk according to the flesh, but according to the Spirit (Galatians 5:16) and to walk by faith and not by sight (2 Corinthians 5:7). But wanting to do this and actually doing this are two very different things. How is this accomplished? In order to defeat the flesh, I needed to be able to distinguish between what is flesh and what is Spirit. God graciously provides the answer through His Spirit and in His Word.

The Flesh

What is the flesh? What I refer to as the flesh is what the Apostle

Paul mentions in Galatians 5:16: "Walk in the Spirit, and you shall not fulfill the lust of the flesh." The Greek word used for flesh here is what is found quite frequently in the New Testament; it can be defined strictly as the meat on your bones, or simply refer to your body as opposed to your soul or spirit; i.e., human nature.8 The flesh is the human nature we inherited from Adam. "Therefore, just as through one man sin entered into the world, and death through sin, and so death spread to all men, because all sinned" (Romans 5:12). From Galatians 5:16, it can be seen that the desires and lusts that we struggle with come from our flesh; it also illustrates the contrast between the flesh and Spirit, and that the two are not compatible. As this is directed to all believers, we all must choose to either live according to our human nature or according to the Spirit.

If our flesh is the source from which our lusts and desires come, that means that our flesh, rather than being tempted by Satan, is what leads us away from God. The flesh loves to get its own way and will rationalize any behavior to get what it wants. Do not be deceived by the flesh. It will try to convince us that we can do something our way, in our time and please the Lord at the same time. When we indulge ourselves, we are indulging the flesh. Since a "little" indulgence seems harmless, we think that it is alright. But it is a lie that we need to indulge ourselves to deal with the stress of life. What we need to indulge in is more of God!

Do not give the flesh any "air time." In other words, don't give it a chance to convince you. The more we dwell on what our flesh wants and is craving, the more we will start to rationalize giving in to it. Once we believe the rationalization that we can get the results we want and still please God (that we can have our way and do it God's way too), we have already turned away from God. Once we do what our flesh wants, our flesh is in control, and it is our master, not the Spirit of God. The more we give in to the flesh, the more entangled we become in it, and the stronger the hold it will have on us. Though it continues to promise peace and joy, all it will ever deliver are temporary thrills followed by emptiness and discontentment – which results in chasing after even more thrills. Following the flesh means getting stuck in this vicious cycle, seeking thrill after thrill that never satisfies. Life lived in the flesh is miserable. There is no meaning to life, only seeking after pleasure (of which there is never enough). We create more misery for ourselves by refusing to say no to the flesh than we ever would experience from being deprived of what the flesh is offering.

The only way to deal with the flesh is to run to God. Talk to God throughout each day; know His Word to be equipped to say NO! and flee from temptation. We may have habitual comforts that we are convinced will mean more misery if we give them up than if we give into them. Wrong. Giving them up **is** hard, but we find that they are not needed after all.

The only reasons for giving up an activity are:

1. It violates an instruction or command in the Word of God;

2. It leads us into sin, or leads someone else into sin. 1 Corinthians 10:23-24 tells us that "All things are lawful for me, but not all things are helpful; all things are lawful for me, but not all things edify. Let no one seek his own, but each one the other's well-being." (See Matthew 18:6 also.)

3. Causes us to become dependent on it for comfort, stress relief, and so forth, rather than on God. To depend on something is to place our trust in it; Proverbs 3:5-6 commands us: "Trust in the Lord with all your heart, and lean not on your own understanding."

The last reason can be the toughest. This is where our flesh really digs its heels in and really puts up a fight. Especially if there isn't anything "wrong" with the activity we are doing. This is where the flesh will try to wear us down with rationalization: "What is wrong with this?" "This isn't hurting anyone!" But the real question is, does this keep us from spending time with God, or from ministering unto others? For even the smallest thing, do we go to God, or do we try to handle it ourselves first? Do we seek a comfort food or activity rather than God? If God is not being considered first, something or someone else is.

Praise God, we have a choice. We do not have to live a life under the burden of the flesh. Christ has made this possible! "For the law of the Spirit of life in Christ Jesus has made me free from the law of sin and of death" (Romans 8:2). While acknowledging Jesus Christ as our Lord and Master may seem as though we are giving up all of our freedom, quite the opposite is true. Life is so much more abundant, precious, joyful and filled with peace, contentment and love when lived in Christ. Rather than losing our freedom, we have gained it, for we have been set free from the bondage and burden of sin. We still have the flesh, temptations to deal with, but we no longer are compelled to serve it. As long as we live in our earthly bodies, temptation is ever with us; but thanks to God, it can no longer enslave us, unless we willingly enslave ourselves to it.

Life is not a drag when lived in the Spirit. On the contrary, when we are in fellowship with God, every activity becomes more meaningful because we do it with Him in mind, and with dependence on Him. We have a choice, then, to either let the flesh convince us that we cannot live without what it desires, or, instead, embrace who and what has been given to us by God and experience God like we never had before. When by His grace we choose to believe that He is better than anything our flesh craves, we find out that not only is He better, He far surpasses anything we can imagine or describe.

While we do not have to obey the flesh, and we are free to live in Christ, once we seek to start living for Christ and in Christ, be forewarned that this only comes supernaturally. Living in the flesh comes naturally. It is like breathing. While we may have the Biblical knowledge of our need to live in Christ, it does not come automatically. As we face inconveniences, trials, and temptations, we are bound to respond in the flesh. It can be very frustrating. If I know it, why am I not living it? Because walking in the Spirit requires submission to, and dependence on, God. "Therefore submit to God. Resist the devil and he will flee from you. Draw near to God and He will draw near to you. Cleanse your hands, you sinners; and purify your hearts, you double-minded." (James 4:7-8)

Submitting to God often means waiting on Him to open or close doors, to reveal His will. This means being willing to let situations go unresolved and to leave the resolution up to Him, in His time. Submitting to God's will also mean putting our trust in Him. Trusting God (faith) means believing that God is good and perfect and will accomplish good even if circumstances at present do not seem to indicate it. Lastly, submitting to God means obeying God. To obey God is to follow the precepts, laws and principles of His Word. Obedience does not mean picking and choosing from Scripture what to follow and what not to follow. It also does not mean adding rules not found in Scripture.

Submission to God, then, is in essence walking by faith and not by sight. The flesh does not like walking by faith, as it requires giving up control, personal comfort, and convenience. Since walking by faith does not come naturally (in the flesh), we can get discouraged and give up, or we can see it as a revelation of our need for God's forgiveness and enabling. The process of dying to self and living in Christ is one in which we discover through each experience that we are unable and He is able; we are weak and He is strong; we are sinful, He is holy. No sooner do we think that we have a handle on something that we fail in that area in some way. God wants to break us of any independence, of any thought that we can accomplish something on our own. Discovering a new need of God is cause for rejoicing! It is another opportunity to trust, rely on, and give glory to God.

Why do we end up doing what we don't want to do? "But each one is tempted when he is drawn away by his own desires and enticed. Then, when desire has conceived, it gives birth to sin" (James 1:14-15a). The desires of the flesh are so enticing because they promise an immediate "feel good" result. But to pursue something just because it feels good makes pleasure our goal, not whatever or whomever is making us feel good. People and activities become a means to an end; people and situations are only sought if they are enjoyable. What is wrong with that? Who doesn't want to feel good? Who doesn't want to feel good, have fun, or experience pleasure?

What is wrong is that when pleasure is pursued, God is not being pursued. It is pleasure that we are serving, not God. It is true that pleasure can be found in what this world offers, but when it becomes our primary focus, it loses its proper context and cannot be fully enjoyed. When pleasure is in focus, whatever activity or person that is producing it is overshadowed by it; the people or actual activity cannot be appreciated for what they are because we are so focused on what we get out of it. This is at the root of the pursuit of pleasure for its own sake: it is all about what we want, not about loving God, loving others and appreciating what God is. It is only when the focus is on God that truly enjoying people and God's gifts is possible.

For each person, what each does to feel good or to cope may be different, but the result is the same: immediate relief that does not solve the problem. There is a solution, however: Jesus said: "Come to me, all ye who labor and are heavy laden and I will give you rest. Take my yoke upon you, and learn from me, for I am gentle and humble in heart and you shall find rest for your souls" (Matthew 11:28-20). To solve the problem of weariness from trying to handle the difficulties of life in and with our own resources, we need to: 1) go to Jesus, 2) take His yoke upon us, and 3) learn from Him.

This sounds simple enough. But the dilemma is this: we must give up seeking our comfort, convenience, and control with the methods that have given us some relief for a solution that promises rest, but no relief from our circumstances. When we don't like the circumstances we are in and we choose to indulge the flesh to feel good, we are in effect saying with our actions that something is better than Jesus and what He has allowed or provided for us. Whatever our circumstances, whether a failing or failed marriage; personal attacks at work, church or home; or loss of job, health, possession or person —they need not to be feared or dreaded. There is **nothing** that can make us miserable, no matter how miserable the circumstances are, if we are looking to and depending on God.

Does our attitude and behavior communicate that Christ is not enough, that what He provides is all well and good, but what we really want is something else? If we are not investing time with the Lord each day in which we are truly present and real with Him, should we be surprised that we are disconnected, that there is staleness to our relationship? The degree to which we experience God and receive spiritual benefit and blessing is the degree to which we submit to Him. If there are areas of our life that we will not give up, they will limit the extent of how much we are going to experience God. If Jesus is not more precious to us than anything else, we need not be surprised when we fall into sin. The only way to develop hatred and distaste for sin and all that the flesh craves is to develop a sweet and precious love for God, Jesus and the Holy Spirit. We are totally dependent on the Lord even for this.

When our hope and delight is found in the Lord, it really does not matter what happens to us down here. When our happiness has its source in the Lord, we do not need new things, going on trips, fun parties, or any other change in circumstance in order to be happy. There is no place or circumstance that we can be in, that God is not there, ever available to us for all that we need. "I will love You, O Lord my strength. The Lord is my rock and my fortress and my deliverer; my God, my strength, in whom I will trust; my shield and the horn of my salvation, my stronghold." (Psalm 18:1-2).

John MacArthur, in his book *The Vanishing Conscience*, gives 10 steps which, if followed, deal with the flesh God's way:

1. Abstain from fleshly lusts

"Beloved, I beg you as sojourners and pilgrims, abstain from fleshly lusts which war against the soul" (1 Peter 2:11); "Flee sexual immorality. Every sin that a man does is outside the body, but he who commits sexual immorality sins against his own body"(1 Corinthians 6:18); "Therefore submit to God. Resist the devil and he will flee from you" (James 4:7).

2. Make no provision for the flesh

"But put on the Lord Jesus Christ, and make no provision for the flesh, to fulfill its lusts" (Romans 13:14).

3. Fix our hearts on Christ

"Beloved, now we are children of God; and it has not yet been revealed what we shall be, but we know that when He is revealed, we shall be like Him, for we shall see Him as He is. And everyone who has this hope in Him purifies himself, just as He is pure" (1 John 3:2-3); But we all, with unveiled face, beholding as in a mirror the glory of the Lord, are being transformed into the same image from glory to glory, just as by the Spirit of the Lord (2 Corinthians 3:18).

4. Mediate on God's Word

"Your word I have hidden in my heart, that I might not sin against You" (Psalm 119:11); "This Book of the Law shall not depart from your mouth, but you shall meditate in it day and night, that you may observe to do according to all that is written in it. For then you will make your way prosperous, and then you will have good success" Josh. 1:8; "Blessed is the man who walks not in the counsel of the ungodly, nor stands in the path of sinners, nor sits in the seat of the scornful; but his delight is in the law of the LORD, and in His law he meditates day and night (Psalm 1:1-2).

5. Pray without ceasing (1 Thessalonians 5:17)

When He came to the place, He said to them, "Pray that you may not enter into temptation" (Luke 22:40); "Watch and pray, lest you enter into temptation. The spirit indeed is willing, but the flesh is weak" (Matthew 26:41).

6. Watch and pray

   "Who can understand his errors? Cleanse me from secret faults. Keep back Your servant also from presumptuous sins; Let them not have dominion over me. Then I shall be blameless, and I shall be innocent of great transgression. Let the words of my mouth and the meditation of my heart be acceptable in Your sight, O LORD, my strength and my Redeemer" (Psalm 19:12-14); "Let us therefore come boldly to the throne of grace, that we may obtain mercy and find grace to help in time of need" (Hebrews 4:16).

7. Exercise self-control

   "But the fruit of the Spirit is love, joy, peace, longsuffering, kindness, goodness, faithfulness, gentleness, self-control. Against such there is no law" (Galatians 5:22-23); "But I discipline my body and bring it into subjection, lest, when I have preached to others, I myself should become disqualified" (1 Corinthians 9:27).

8. Be filled with the Holy Spirit

   "And do not be drunk with wine, in which is dissipation; but be filled with the Spirit," (Ephesians 5:18). MacArthur comments: "In other words, God both molds our wills to obey and then gives us the energy to work according to whatever pleases Him. That is the Spirit-filled life."

9. Clothe yourself with humility

   "Likewise you younger people, submit yourselves to your elders. Yes, all of you be submissive to one another, and be clothed with humility, for 'God resists the proud, but gives grace to the humble'"

(1 Peter 5:5). "Let this mind be in you which was also in Christ Jesus" (Philippians 2:5).

10. Put on the armor of God (Ephesians 6:11-17)

"Walk in the Spirit, and you will not carry out the desire of the flesh" (Galatians 5:16)

"Therefore, having these promises, beloved, let us cleanse ourselves from all filthiness of the flesh and spirit, perfecting holiness in the fear of God." (2 Corinthians 7:1)[9]

Again, we are completely dependent on God's grace to accomplish this. What the flesh wants (what we crave) gives us a temporary "fix," but it never leads to contentment, happiness, peace, or joy. "Many people seek happiness and never find it because it is never found when you seek it directly ... we must see joy as a by-product of obedience."[10] All we need is God and what He gives us through and by His Son and by His Spirit.

Is what we do, view, or hear, feeding the flesh and starving the Spirit or starving the flesh and feeding the Spirit? Remember: there is nothing that feeds the flesh in the Word of God. Does what we are doing encourage, support and enable us to be more God-centered instead of self-centered? If we continually choose to feed the flesh, is it any surprise our relationship with God is suffering? Does what I am choosing to see, hear, and do keep me from enjoying God?

Instead of making it all about what we want, make it all about God. Remember that getting what our flesh wants is something that is never completely obtained.

It isn't getting what we want

But how we receive what we get;

It isn't rejoicing in the gift,

But in the Giver.

For even when we get want our flesh wants,

And we think that we'll be satisfied –

There always remains something lacking

And we continually long for more.

Satisfaction only comes from God, whom our spirit longs for. We cannot live on past victories or on lessons we have learned. To walk in the Spirit requires a tender heart that is eager to repent of anything that prevents fellowship.

We are able, and are commanded, to put the deeds of the flesh to death; we cannot, however, put the flesh to death (Romans 8:13). "For to be carnally minded is death but to be spiritually minded is life and peace." (Romans 8:6) "I say then, walk in the Spirit, and you shall not fulfill the lust of the flesh." (Galatians 5:15).

Walking in the Spirit does not remove the flesh or any part of it. As long as we have these earthly, cursed bodies, we will have the flesh to contend with. But we are not bound to serve it. Christ has set us free from the chains of sin and death! (Romans 8:2) But having been set free from the bondage of sin and death, the flesh is still with us.

What about this flesh? How do we recognize what is flesh and what is Spirit? Other than sins we knowingly commit, how is the flesh manifested? It is manifested in bondage to meeting emotional needs through intellectual or physical means: the intellect creates strategies or fantasies; physical lusts or concerns create emotional needs demanding immediate resolution.

Let's take a look, then, at the three components of the flesh: emotion, desire, and intellect.

Emotion

"Brethren, join in following my example, and note those who so walk, as you have us for a pattern. For many walk, of whom I have told you often, and now tell you even weeping, that they are the enemies of the cross of Christ: whose end is destruction, whose god is their belly, and whose glory is in their shame—who set their mind on earthly things." (Philippians 3:17-19)

"Help me to honor thee by believing before I feel, for great is the sin if I make feeling a cause of faith."[11]

Part of our human nature or our flesh that we have to live with every day is our emotions. Emotions are a reaction to external or internal stimuli. They may be a reaction to stress, other people, circumstances, etc., or they may be a result of being sick or a hormonal imbalance.

Our emotions can mislead us; they cannot be relied upon. That does not mean that emotions are wrong or evil—it is not wrong to be happy or sad, bored or fearful. We cannot control the way we feel, but it becomes sin when our feelings rule us. When emotions are in control, the most intelligent person will become irrational and illogical. No matter how much education we have, how high our IQ, or how capable we are, when our emotions are in control, they determine what we accept or do not accept. Our understanding of reality and our approach to life will not be based on what is true, but on what we **feel** is right. Our feelings become the rule by which we live and evaluate other people and our environment. Right and wrong is not determined by what God says, but by our feelings. "My conscience is clear" means that we have not done wrong because we do not feel that we have done wrong. A theme often heard in popular songs is "how can it be wrong when it feels so right?"

We cannot control the way we feel, but we can determine how we will act. When we allow our feelings to determine what we do, it is sin; we serve it rather than God. We cannot be ruled by God and ruled by emotion ("You cannot serve two masters" Matthew 6:24).

We can get so caught up in our emotions that other people's feelings are not considered. Getting our work done, honoring God, doing what is right can fall by the wayside when we are focused on enjoying ourselves and having a good time. Giving enjoyment top priority is serving the flesh, ourselves. It is not serving God first. To chase after pleasure is vanity, "I said in my heart, 'Come now, I will test you with mirth; therefore enjoy pleasure'; but surely, this also was vanity" (Ecclesiastes 2:1).

We are more familiar with how negative emotions lead to sin: bitterness, anger, depression, fearfulness. Bitterness comes from hurt that has not healed and not forgiven; anger, from a sense of injustice or injury; emotional depression, from anger over circumstances; fear from the potential of getting hurt (often seen in worry). Gossip, backbiting, rudeness, stinginess are a few more sins that come from an emotional reaction. Whatever sin it is, it is rooted in our emotional response to either our circumstances or other people in our lives.

How we deal with that emotional response directly impacts our spiritual life. We can either focus on how we feel, or we can choose to trust God with how we feel, and believe His way is for our best, including having these emotions. Focusing on ourselves, on how we feel, or on our circumstances, will always result in misery. If we are in fellowship with God, there is joy and peace, despite whatever pain we are experiencing.

Doing things His way does not mean ignoring or denying or stamping down how we feel. Am I afraid, fearful? "Whenever I am afraid, I will trust in You" (Psalm 56:3). Am I angry or hurt? "Be kind to one another, tenderhearted, forgiving one another, even as God in Christ forgave you"

(Ephesians 4:32). Am I depressed? "Why are you cast down, O my soul? ... Hope thou in God..." (Psalm 42:5). Handling our emotions God's way means being honest about how we feel, acknowledging why we feel that way, then laying it at His feet. It is being willing to do whatever is needed to deal with the root of the emotional problem: to repent of our sin when that is causing it, or forgiving someone else if we have been wronged.

When we simply try to cope with our emotions, rather that to get to the root, we cope with what the flesh prefers: food, sex, drugs, cleaning, work, sports, entertainment, or fantasy. Giving in to what the flesh is craving may seem to provide relief, but any "relief" that is felt is temporary. Rather than providing any real relief, any "solution" the flesh provides can only create a desire for more relief and further pursuit of its desires, which only adds another (sin) problem. This is all the more reason to deal with our feelings God's way, and not according to the flesh.

If we are depressed or anxious, or have severe mood swings, and cannot trace our emotional response to a person or event, the cause may be spiritual in nature rather than physical. Prayer will reveal this, for when we ask God to reveal any sin at the root of our emotional response, He will. It also may be helpful to go to another believer who we trust for a more objective view of the situation. If there still remains a problem, we may need medical counsel. But if the cause is spiritual, not physical, medication is only going to enable denial and self-deception, and the problem will only be exasperated. Something that only helps us feel better, but doesn't deal with the root of the problem, is no help at all.

I have experienced a long period of depression myself; if I had sought medication, I would never have come to realize that the root of the depression was spiritual. I could not see what the root of my depression was until God revealed it to me. "He also brought me up out of a horrible pit, out of the miry clay, and set my feet upon a rock, and established my steps" (Psalm

4):2). Until I repented of seeking something other than God, and realized that there wasn't anything better than Him, I did not recover from my depression. Medication would not have helped me at all. **But** there are physical causes for depression and other emotional difficulties and we need to prayerfully consider what the course of action should be. "I waited patiently for the LORD, and He inclined to me, and He heard my cry" (Psalm 40:1).

When the source of the emotional problem is not physical, it is important to understand from the outset that we cannot work out emotional problems through intellectual means. We cannot count on our ability to think through problems or make good decisions when our emotions are controlling us. The only way to handle emotion is through spiritual means. When I was going through depression, I kept trying to find the solution through intellectual means (analysis). Analyzing our feelings does not solve any problems; it does the exact opposite. By focusing on how we feel, we are pouring more energy into our emotions, intensifying them rather than finding relief.

Even though I earnestly sought the Lord on a daily basis, I kept asking for the wrong thing. I wanted what I thought would make me happy. I kept asking for blessing, for certain things to be given to me. Since I did not get what I wanted, I became confused as well as depressed! I thought that the Lord was being unkind, unfair, that I was being punished. I knew that God is good, loving, just, and holy; but this was not jiving with what He was allowing to happen. The depression was not resolved until I stopped trying to figure it out. With the gracious help of His Spirit, I came to the realization that the problem was not with God, but with me and my expectations. When I came to the end of myself, and my attempts to figure things out, and humbled myself before the Lord, He helped me see my sin: that my focus was on the gifts and not on the Giver (God). I needed to see and know that God is better than anything my flesh could possibly want or this world could ever offer. Contentment, joy, peace, and satisfaction are not found in relationships with others or in circumstances; they are only found in God.

What then, are the spiritual means of dealing with our emotions? Obedience is the key. It is running straight to God and running directly away from selfish desires. It means owning our bankrupt state before God and receiving His abundant mercy and grace. Dealing with emotions God's way requires two things happening at once; believing God and disbelieving our emotions. No matter how our emotions convince us that we must have this or we must do that, IT IS NOT SO. Only Jesus Christ is the way, truth, and life (John 14:6). Our emotions cannot be given more credit than they are due. They cannot ever correctly perceive or evaluate; all they can do is feel. The only way our relationship with God can be properly evaluated is with the Word of God. To use emotions, not His Word, leads to worshipping and serving something other than God. That is why we must trust God and what He tells us in His Word despite what out feelings are telling us.

When circumstances test our faith, remember what God has done for us: "But God demonstrates His own love toward us, in that while we were yet sinners, Christ died for us" (Rom. 5:8); "I am the good Shepherd" (John 10:11); "...the Lord is gracious: (I Peter 2:3); "...His righteousness endures forever...The Lord is gracious and compassionate" (Psalm 111:3-4); and "... ascribe greatness to our God, He is the Rock, His work is perfect; for all His ways are justice, a God of truth and without injustice; righteous and upright is He." (Deuteronomy 32:3-4). The truth of God's Word will reveal the lies that our emotions tell us.

There are also helpful, practical ways of dealing with emotions, such as physical exercise, talking with a friend, writing, working, artistic outlets, and so forth. All of these will have some measure of success; but in dealing with the source or root of the problem, **reading God's Word** and **prayer** are essential.

Reading the Word of God is first and foremost an encounter with God. His Word not only reveals intellectual truth about Him, it is "God-breathed" (2 Timothy 3:16) and it is the vehicle by which the Spirit of God communicates with us. His Word reminds us of what is true (God) and that feelings are not a standard for truth.

Prayer is the means by which we express our need for God and are ministered to by Him. But we won't see our need for Him if we have not seen our own inability to meet our needs our way. Prayer is the means by which we align our wills with God's will. "Now this is the confidence that we have in Him, that if we ask anything according to His will, He hears us" (I John 5:14).

It is important that we do not gloss over, ignore, suppress or express our feelings inappropriately. We have learned to respond emotionally through culture, family, or from times when we have been personally attacked by others. We may have been made to feel that we have overreacted, were too sensitive, etc. so we "toughened up." We may have learned that emotional displays of any kind were not desired or accepted. Neither is a biblical or Godly response. God's Word tells us to "be angry, and do not sin" (Ephesians 4:26). Anger is not a sin – it is what we do with it that is or is not sinful, and this is true of all our emotions. How we feel does matter—but the solution to resolving hurt, anxiety, fear or anger is not withdrawal, passive resistance, or retaliation, dumping on others, using foul language or violent behavior. (The flesh wants immediate gratification.) The solution to resolving any emotional issue is to do exactly what the flesh does not want to do: surrender any attempt to cope with it ourselves, and humble ourselves before the Lord.

To not pay attention to what we are feeling, or to ignore it, is to do so at our own peril. When we have a negative emotional response, or an inappropriate positive one, those are means by which God has given us to tell us that something is wrong, and that we need to go to Him. Obedience is not just "coping," the "stiff upper lip" approach. This may give the appearance that we are pleasing the Lord, but it may be that we are only doing it out of a sense of duty, not out of love for Him. A right response to negative emotions is to take them to Him, so that the cause can be determined. If our emotion is a fleshly response (which is usually the case), we can then lay it before the Lord and trust Him to enable us to do what is right despite how we feel. Then, obedience is no longer what we **have** to do, but what we **want** to do.

How does this truth apply when we are faced with stressful situations or strong emotions? Do we just ignore or suppress how we feel? This is not the solution, for God loves us and cares about how we feel; He also knows much more than we do about the purpose of the trial (test of faith) and how we will benefit from it. When overwhelmed with emotion, we must not either over-emphasize or de-emphasize feelings, but simply state what the feeling is and ask for comfort, peace, and strength to do His will. Our first impulse is to pray that God will make us feel better, either by changing our emotions or our circumstances. While we may think that getting rid of difficult emotions is the solution, our real need is to focus on God instead of our feelings, trusting God to enable us to do this. Because emotions are the result of stimuli, they will respond to obedience to God positively, and to self-centeredness negatively.

This seems like a simple solution, but it is difficult to apply. I have come running to God, only to be distracted by the flesh once again. Learning dependence on God is a lifelong process, because that is how long we have the flesh to contend with. We are used to dealing with life's problems (stress, boredom) on our own. We go to God when our resources fail us, when we should have gone to Him in the first place. The flesh always seeks immediate relief from even the slightest physical or emotional pain. The difficulty is learning to accept being uncomfortable, inconvenienced, or even to suffer for the sake of waiting upon God, and being willing to believe that His solution, grace, and strength is much, much better than immediate relief and gratification.

This is only possible with God. He will reveal whether we are living in the flesh or in the Spirit; then the choice is ours to humble ourselves, asking for help and forgiveness. God's Word is "living and powerful, sharper than any two-edged sword, piercing even to the division of soul and spirit, of both joints and marrow, and is a discerner of the thoughts and intents of the heart" (Hebrews 4:12).

We are without excuse for the choices we make. To blame other people, circumstances, or lack of knowledge for our behavior is to only deceive ourselves. It is only when we willingly look into the mirror of the Word, see the error and sin that is revealed, and repent, that we will experience the freedom that is in Jesus Christ.

A very real danger for believers is refusing to believe unless they **feel** something is true, that is, that God isn't "in" something unless they "feel" Him present in it. They assume that since they are a new creation in Christ, their new nature will manifest itself in its own time, as they "feel" led by the Spirit. Commands and directives from Scripture are ignored, or re-interpreted as not applying to them. Yet if this is true, why are we told in Colossians to "put on tender mercies..." (3:12)? Would it be necessary to "put on" if they were already "on?" Clearly, we cannot wait until we "feel" led or "feel" like walking in the Spirit; this is a choice we must make, depending on God, despite how we feel.

Why do we bring physical needs or circumstantial problems to God in prayer, but rarely pray for guidance in dealing with our emotions? Is the reason for this that deep down we do not trust God to provide for our emotional needs? Are we afraid that He would allow something potentially hurtful or frightening into our lives? Thinking that we need to have certain things, circumstances, or people in our lives in order to be happy is a trap we all fall into. God wants us to see and realize that **He** is the source for emotional stability: comfort, peace, and joy. "But the fruit of the spirit is love, joy, peace..." (Galatians 5:22a).

Once we make this choice and continue in it, we begin to know God and to love Him for the greater love He bestows on us. We hate our sin and anything that leads us away from Him. The more we love Him, the more we want to experience Him, His presence. When we love Him, no motivation is needed for good works. We are already motivated to serve Him and honor Him. This is what is meant by "If you love me, keep my commandments" (John 14:15). We do not need any "feel good" sermons; Christ surpasses anything we can imagine.

Who or what can compare to the love, grace, comfort, healing, and strength that only God gives? Who is as awesome, holy, faithful, and long-suffering as He is?

Desires (Lusts of the flesh)

"But put on the Lord Jesus Christ, and make no provision for the flesh, to fulfill its lusts" (Romans 13:14).

Emotions also play a part in our struggle with physical desires. When our physical desires demand satisfaction, not getting it will result in an emotional response. We have discussed our emotional responses to outward stimuli, namely, circumstances and people. Here the focus will be how we deal with desires or lusts of the flesh, and any emotions that result.

A desire that seeks something that only gives a momentary, temporary pleasure and gratification is of the flesh, and not of God. A desire of the flesh that can rule us is hunger. Food, if we let it, can become our god. When we are craving a certain food, giving into the temptation to eat (when we are not really hungry), will not satisfy the craving, but make it worse. This is always the way of the flesh. Instead of satisfaction, it causes more craving. In the end, we are left weary and heavy-laden. 1 Corinthians 6:13 reminds us that "Foods for the stomach and the stomach for foods, but God will destroy both it and them. Now the body is not for sexual immorality but for the Lord, and the Lord for the body."

Gluttony is one of the least mentioned and overlooked sins. Is it an indication of the lack of discipline in other areas of our lives? Have we submitted to the Lord in almost everything else but this? Whatever reason there may be for over-indulgence, food is meant to be a means to an end, not an end in and of itself. A prayer that addresses food with a God-honoring attitude will say: "Bless this food to our bodies for Your (God's) service."

As children of God who love Him, we want to have this attitude. But when we are accustomed to a certain way of eating, or accustomed to certain foods that we enjoy (and depend on for emotional relief), we will find out very quickly how dependent we have become when we attempt to give it up or alter it in any way. This is an eye-opener, alerting us to the fact that we have been allowing our physical appetite to control us, instead of being controlled by the Holy Spirit. When the flesh is used to getting what it wants, it will put up a real fight when we submit to the Spirit instead of yielding to the flesh.

Are we eating that which will only increase our appetite (make us want to eat more) or are we eating that which will satisfy? Are we willing to accept the body God has given us and be thankful for it? Are we eating when we don't need to? Are we eating because we can; do we eat until we cannot eat any more? It is not a matter of how much we can eat, or getting as much as we can of what is good; it is a matter of only eating as much as we physically need. For us who are children of God, our bodies are the temple of the Holy Spirit (1 Corinthians 6:19) – to eat more than we need is neglecting to take care of the body God has given us. Are we going to obey the desire or impulse for more, or are we going to follow the God-given sensation of true hunger, and only eat when we really need to eat? Is our hunger, desire for food, our god? "For many walk, of whom I have told you often, and now tell you even weeping, that they are the enemies of the cross of Christ: whose end is destruction, whose god is their belly, and whose glory is in their shame —who set their mind on earthly things" (Philippians 3:18-19). Once food is consumed to satisfy the lust of the flesh, or to give us pleasure or fill some emotional need, we are not depending on God or His Spirit, but on the flesh. If we have to have what we want, when we want it, it has become our god, which is idolatry. Serving anything or anyone else other than God is sin.

Though I am primarily focusing on those who overeat, or do not eat healthy foods, there are those who are obsessed with food, but for a different reason. Instead of eating too much, they will purposely not eat enough (anorexic) or those who eat and then throw up (bulimic). These do not seem to have anything in common with gluttony, but both are an obsession with food. Whether we overeat or don't eat enough, we are being controlled by the flesh. Those who overeat are dependent on the pleasure that they get from food; those who don't eat are convinced by the flesh that they are in control by controlling their eating behaviors, and are just as dependent emotionally on not eating as the person is who does eat. Either problem is rooted in meeting emotional needs; it is simply being manifested in different ways.

The flesh can be diabolical. Just when we think that we have surrendered to the Lord, the need for control can rear its ugly head. For example: we have an addiction to sugar and decide to remove it from the diet. But we don't stop there. It leads to more and more restriction; we start to be controlled by fear of everything that might be harmful for us and go to extremes in what we will eat and not eat. We will find ourselves serving the flesh's need for control: believing that we can control everything we put into our mouths, ensuring emotional and physical equilibrium, and preventing disease. Such a belief puts confidence in our strength, not in the Lord. "It is better to trust in the LORD than to put confidence in man" (Psalm 118:8). God has also not given us a "spirit of fear, but of power, and of love, and of a sound mind" (2 Timothy 1:7). While we are to be good stewards of our bodies, God never meant for us to seek protection or security through our own means; that is idolatry. The proper balance is to be a good steward of our bodies, and not to worry about the future or every possible disease that is out there. Walking by faith requires trusting that God will take care of us in sickness and in health; He is our healer—either now on earth or with Him in glory!

Food, whether we love it or hate it, can be an instrument the flesh uses to lead us down the path of self-destruction: both extremes—gluttony or anorexia—result in the destruction of the body. Just like any other device of the flesh, whatever coping mechanisms they provide ultimately fail. We can never eat enough food to completely meet our emotional needs; increasingly greater and greater amounts must be eaten to achieve any enjoyment. Then we can never be thin enough. No matter how much we exercise or how much we deny ourselves, we will never be happy with our bodies. The only solution in either situation is to recognize the failure of a fleshly solution, and seek what only God can provide instead! For those who are in a stronghold, stopping will be very difficult. Support is needed from a pastor or biblical counselor. "Brethren, if a man is overtaken in any trespass, you who are spiritual, restore such a one in a spirit of gentleness" (Galatians 6:2).

Although I have mainly focused on gluttony, the principles apply to any desire of the flesh; whatever we are convinced we need in order to be satisfied. But the flesh cannot ever properly perceive what it needs! So what do we do when we are in a situation in which we have a desire that is unfulfilled (and God isn't supplying it)? We have a choice: to believe that going without it is for our good, and we will be better off, or to assume that God "needs our help" and go about fulfilling that desire ourselves, which is sin.

To say no to fleshly desires when it is comfort or control that we want will feel as though we are going against our nature; we are not being true to ourselves. We **are** going against our nature—our fleshly, sinful nature. But our **true** identity is that we are a child of God, not of the flesh or any of the feelings or desires that accompany it. We are now a new creation: "Therefore, if anyone is in Christ, he is a new creation; old things have passed away, all things have become new." What old things? What does this mean? We know that it cannot mean that our old nature, sinful nature (flesh) has been taken away and that we have been given a new sinless one. Otherwise, there would be no need for Paul to command believers to "put off, concerning your former conduct, the old man" and "be renewed in the spirit of your mind" (Ephesians 4:22-23).

The "old things" that "have passed away" is referring to the old order of things. Before we were saved, we were in bondage to sin: "For we know that the law is spiritual, but I am carnal, sold under sin"(Romans 7:14); we could not choose to walk by the Spirit of God. When Christ saved us, He removed us from the bondage of sin and death. "For the law of the Spirit of life in Christ Jesus has made me free from the law of sin and death" (Romans 8:2). When a person is saved, the old order (bondage to sin) has passed away; a new order has been given (bondage to Christ). "For you were bought at a price; therefore glorify God in your body and in your spirit, which are God's" (1 Corinthians 6:20). We are now free to choose to depend, trust and obey God.

The only desires that are characteristic of our identity in Christ Jesus are desires to love, honor, and obey God in all things. If we live according to the Spirit, and not according to the flesh, we claim the identity that we have been given in Christ. When we submit ourselves to God, God can then transform us into the image of Christ. "...Being confident of this very thing, that He who began a good work in you will complete it until the day of Jesus Christ" (Philippians 1: 6). Refusing to die to selfish desires of the flesh means never living out our true identity.

Being a new creature in Christ does not mean we simply stop one behavior and replace it with another. It is not simply about behavior modification, but about whom we are serving. Nor does being a new creation in Christ mean that when God sets us free from the bondage to sin, that it is now up to us to transform ourselves into the image of Christ. Such an approach results in self-reliance, independence, and arrogance, which is the antithesis of walking in the Spirit.

But independence, self-sufficiency, or freedom is exactly what our flesh will demand. To be a slave, to have been bought, feels like service is being forced, that it is a burden. Human nature (i.e. the flesh) hates the idea of being owned. We live in a country that demands its freedoms; men have fought and died for it. Where is freedom as a Christian if we are a slave?

Here is the irony of it: while it is true that we are God's property (Jesus paid the price for us), He is not a master that forces obedience. We have a choice. We will face consequences for our sin; but we do not "have to" do anything. We hate the idea of losing our freedom; a loss of it creates feelings of entrapment, forced servitude. But if we are really honest, we hate the loss of freedom because our flesh wants to do what it wants to do, when it wants to do it. The flesh will seek to have its way, as long and as frequently as we will choose to follow it. Anytime that this choice is made is a choice to rebel against God and His way.

Our feelings and desires lead us astray when they become the means **by which we define who we are**. As desires come from a corrupted flesh, and emotions are reactions to either that which is of God or that which is not, we cannot define who we are by what we feel. When we find our identity through either our desires or feelings, it will result in us identifying with our flesh rather than with who we are in Christ Jesus. As we obey the Spirit, our feelings will change: what we did not feel like doing before, we are now glad that we do. When our focus is on meeting our desires, it is a continual pursuit in a race in which there is no finish line; there is immediate gratification, but no satisfaction. This is where the irony comes in. Giving in to what we physically want only increases the desire for that object or activity. When desires are obeyed and pursued, they control us.

What if the desire we have is for a child, or for a husband/wife? Many argue that God has given us the desire for these things, therefore He will provide. But when He doesn't, we put our lives on hold (not really living), or we try to make it happen. In this situation we have to ask ourselves: is what I want more important than knowing and serving God? If so, that desire is of the flesh and not of the Spirit. While recognizing this does not get rid of the desire, it does help us to see that if God has not made it happen, it is either not the right time, or it is not for our good. Husband or children may be a natural desire, but it may not be what God uses to accomplish our sanctification, which is His will for us (1 Thessalonians 4:3).

This is when our faith is tested: when we really, really want something, and God has not provided it for us, and we are left with intense feelings and desires for that thing. At this point the question is are we going to trust that God loves us and is doing what is best for us, even if He is not providing it? In dealing with intense desires and feelings, it is easy to question God's goodness and His love for us. Fleshly desires by their very nature never satisfy, cast doubt on God's provision, and deceive us.

Dwelling on our desires exaggerates and blows them out of proportion. No matter how intense a desire is, **it is lying to us**. Not only can we live without whatever we think we have to have, we can be happy without it. "God is our refuge and strength" (Psalm 46:1); without Him, there would be nothing to live for, life would be without meaning. How I thank God that this struggle with the flesh is not for nothing! In struggling against the flesh I learn how insufficient and lacking the flesh is and more and more of how great and wonderful God is, and how He alone satisfies.

Intense desires and feelings can be very difficult to deal with. When we feel strongly, we strongly believe what we are feeling. Dealing with these intense desires or feelings requires two things: dependence on God and a renewed mind. "...Be transformed by the renewing of your mind, that you may prove what is that good and acceptable and perfect will of God" (Romans 12:2). The latter is accomplished by saturating our minds with the Word of God, and choosing to obey it in regards to what we think about, view, hear, and do. But to attempt to live according to the Word of God without dependence on God is to battle fleshly desires with fleshly strength. The flesh

Why Am I So Miserable If This is the Lord's Will

will always fail us; God never fails. Obedience without dependence on God does not work, for we cannot do things His way and do them our way at the same time. Pleasing God can only be accomplished according to His way and means. "The LORD *is* righteous in her midst, He will do no unrighteousness. Every morning He brings His justice to light; He never fails, but the unjust knows no shame" (Zephaniah 3:5). To deal with these desires, we must first recognize that the battle is with the flesh and that the only solution is to run straight to God for the supernatural help and strength that we need.

Turn back to God, and remember that we belong to **Him**. Those who are saved by grace through faith are His children. We do not need to go looking for Him; He is right here, and has been here the whole time we were chasing after something else that promised to be better than what He was providing. We need to return to Him.

Prayer, Bible reading, or any other spiritual exercise is not going to be what we feel like doing when we are struggling with intense desires and feelings. Usually, we are so miserable that the idea of doing anything that is not pleasing to the flesh is repulsive. There is a reason for this: as we grow in Christ, and start saying no to fleshly desires, we are, in effect, going through withdrawal. Our flesh is used to getting what it wants to cope or feel better. Once we stop living according to flesh, and start walking according to the Spirit, we can count on our flesh not giving up quietly. But no matter how loudly it protests, to believe it is to be deceived. The flesh can never give us satisfaction, peace, joy, goodness, love, perfection, contentment, or anything else that God gives.

The Apostle Paul expressed in Colossians 2:20-22: "Therefore, if you died with Christ from the basic principles of the world, why, as though living in the world, do you subject yourselves to regulations— 'Do not touch, do not taste, do not handle,' which all concern things which perish with the using —according to the commandments and doctrines of men?" We must also be careful that we do not let ourselves be ruled by any regulations that we or someone else creates, but that everything we do is to please God not man.

When we recognize that a desire of the flesh is a problem for us, what do we do? First, pray. Pray that God will enable us to recognize the lies that our flesh, the world, or Satan is telling us, and confront them with His truth. What truth? That whatever our flesh desires does not, will not, and cannot satisfy us emotionally or spiritually. Also, that the flesh cannot be reformed; our fleshly desires will try to bargain with us, so that we will compromise and not deny them completely. It will protest that giving up what it wants is too hard and will claim that what we get for giving it up doesn't measure up to what we get for giving in to it. But it cannot be bargained with. It must be denied. In order to deny the flesh, prayer and utter dependence on God are essential. We need to remember our absolute poverty and need for God and pray for his grace, strength and wisdom. We must remember that **anything** the flesh craves falls way short of anything God provides for us.

As long as we live in these bodies, these desires that lead us away from God and do not satisfy do not go away. While this is true, they will control us only if we allow them to. "No temptation has overtaken you except such as is common to man: but God is faithful, who will not allow you to be tempted beyond what you are able, but with temptation will also make the way of escape, that you may be able to bear it" (1 Corinthians 10:13). If we give in to temptation, this does not mean that God has failed us! It means that no matter how strong our desires, He will enable us to deny them and obey Him. God also provides this counsel from His Word, which, if followed, will keep us from dwelling on our feelings and desires: "Finally brethren, whatever are true, whatever things are noble, whatever things are just, whatever things are pure, whatever things are lovely, whatever things are of good repute, if there is any virtue and if there is anything praiseworthy—meditate on these things" (Philippians 4:8).

Our chief enjoyment will always come from knowing Him; everything else is best enjoyed for the glory it gives to God. The pleasures of the flesh will destroy us. It is not that we hate any of the good things God provides for us to enjoy, but a dependency on them can often lead to sin. What God provides for our enjoyment is meant to be the icing on the cake, not the cake. The bottom line is: does it ultimately lead us away from God? No matter how appealing it might be to the flesh, or how harmless the activity may appear, if it distracts us from our relationship with God, it is sin! It is against us, and will prevent us from having the abundant life that only Christ can provide. When God is our focus, when we depend on Him, when we find our satisfaction in Him, what the flesh offers pales by comparison. When we do experience God, we find that "… partially enjoying God is better than fully enjoying anything else."[12]

Intellect

"I beseech you therefore, brethren, by the mercies of God, that you present your bodies a living sacrifice, holy, acceptable to God, which is your reasonable service. And do not be conformed to this world, but be transformed by the renewing of your mind, that you may prove what is that good and acceptable and perfect will of God." (Romans 12:1-2).

The third component of the flesh is our intellect. While some rely on what they feel (emotions) for the decisions they make, or to determine what they believe, there are others who rely on knowledge and understanding in order to believe or to apply that belief.

Does understanding why we sin really keep us from sinning? It will only give us an excuse to sin. To eliminate that excuse is futile, for once the excuse is eliminated, another takes its place. The desire of the flesh will always give us a reason to sin. "Where do wars and fights come from among you? Do they not come from your desires for pleasure that war in your members?" (James 4:1).

2 Corinthians 10:3 tells us clearly that "though we walk in the flesh, we do not war according to the flesh." The battle against sin cannot be won emotionally, intellectually, or with any physical desire. Using analysis is a weapon of the flesh. It also provides an excuse for dwelling on something the flesh enjoys dwelling on: sin. Verse 5 of the same chapter tells us what we need to do: "bringing every thought into captivity to the obedience of Christ."

Do not be surprised when desires tempt you. Do not think that they can be handled in our own strength. They can't. No measure of human strength is able to handle them. There is no reasoning with them; there is no reforming the flesh. The deeds of the flesh must be put to death (Romans 8:13). The only way to deal with the lures, temptations, and desires of the flesh is to flee from them and not to feed those appetites. The more we try to figure out how to defeat some sin with strategies, plans, or analysis, the more entrenched we become. We have to turn from them to God; we need to repent.

As soon as we realize that we are pursuing sin or a desire of the flesh, we must **stop**. Whatever it is we are thinking, seeing, tasting, touching, hearing, doing or saying, if it is sin; don't try to rationalize it or make excuses! Drop it and run to Christ!

Because we don't want to sin, we feel obligated to try to find a solution. But this is exactly what encourages self-reliance and feeds the flesh. The battle with the flesh cannot be won with any natural weapon; the only weapons that work are supernatural — the armor of God:

"Finally, my brethren, be strong in the Lord and in the power of His might. Put on the whole armor of God, that you may be able to stand

against the wiles of the devil. For we do not wrestle against flesh and blood, but against principalities, against powers, against the rulers of the darkness of this age, against spiritual hosts of wickedness in the heavenly places. Therefore take up the whole armor of God, that you may be able to withstand in the evil day, and having done all, to stand.

"Stand therefore, having girded your waist with truth, having put on the breastplate of righteousness, and having shod your feet with the preparation of the gospel of peace; above all, taking the shield of faith with which you will be able to quench all the fiery darts of the wicked one. And take the helmet of salvation, and the sword of the Spirit, which is the word of God; praying always with all prayer and supplication in the Spirit, being watchful to this end with all perseverance and supplication for all the saints" (Ephesians 6: 10-18).

Our spiritual weapons for dealing with the flesh, temptation, and sin are: 1) salvation; 2) truth (the Word of God); 3) righteousness (given at salvation); 4) the gospel (again, His Word); 5) faith; lastly, but not least, 6) prayer. To have victory over the flesh, sin, Satan, or temptation, we must be born again of the Spirit of God, live in submission to Him, know His Word, and pray always. The flesh will deceive us into thinking that if we could only understand why we sin we could prevent it (whatever it is) from happening again. All the knowledge and understanding in the world does not keep us from sinning; only trusting, obeying, and depending on God, while resting on the promises of His Word will bring spiritual victory. No man-made argument or strategy can ever accomplish sanctification.

The need to understand is an intellectual pitfall of the flesh. Another is the belief that what we already have learned will ensure spiritual success. 1

Corinthians 13:2 tells us: "though I have the gift of prophecy, and understand all mysteries and all knowledge, and though I have all faith, so that I could remove mountains, but have not love, I am nothing." Knowledge without a love for God and a love for others will always lead to pride, legalism, and self-righteousness. It will never produce anything of eternal value that will glorify God.

Biblical knowledge is different from any other knowledge. Hebrews 4:12 states: "For the word of God is living and powerful, and sharper than any two-edged sword, piercing even to the division of soul and spirit, and of joints and marrow, and is a discerner of the thoughts and intents of the heart." But unfortunately, the Word of God can be misused; it can be misrepresented and taken out of context. It can be treated simply as a textbook and not given significance over other books (treated casually or irreverently), or treated like a formula, which if followed gives us what we want. If any of these take place, then the knowledge which it provides is not going to have the proper application. To focus on God's Word thinking that it is the same as focusing on Him is to run the danger of not only loving truth at the expense of others, but creating our own version of His truth. Another version of His truth isn't God's truth at all.

But if the Word of God is "living and powerful" (Hebrews 4:12), how is it that not everyone is impacted by it when they hear it or read it? God's Word also tells us that "...faith comes by hearing, and hearing by the word of God." (Romans 10:17) But Christ also addressed the crowds with the admonition: "He who has ears to hear, let him hear!" (Matthew 11:15) Who is going to have the ears to hear? Ephesians 2:8-9 tells us that it is by God's grace that we are saved, that it is a gift of God; we cannot do any work that accomplishes our salvation. Clearly those who hear are able to hear by the grace of God.

What about those who have accepted Christ as Savior and yet do not seem to be impacted by God's Word, or who knowingly misuse the Word?

Either they think they are saved and are not; or they are saved, but out of fellowship with God. If there is known or unknown sin, it will block fellowship with God, and thereby hinder the impact of the Word of God. That is why prayer and reading the Word need to go together—always. We need to prepare our hearts and minds with prayer, before approaching the Word of God, confessing any known sin and asking for any unknown sin to be revealed and for the right attitude.

Claiming to love God's Word and not putting God first in our lives (not loving God with our whole heart, mind, and strength) can lead one to become a legalist. When God is not given first place, what we define as truth, as what is right, is not going to be based on God, but on our own understanding. Proverbs 12:15 defines this behavior as foolish: "the way of a fool is right in his own eyes, but he who heeds counsel is wise." When truth is defined by our understanding, what we define as right becomes law; anyone who does not live up to it is wrong and is therefore under our condemnation, disapproval, or rejection. In so doing we become the authority and demonstrate a lack of love for God and others.

The flesh is confident in itself, not in the Lord. Intellectually, this is manifested by being confident in what a person knows and understands. The Apostle Paul sets the example by stating: "For we are the circumcision, who worship God in the Spirit, rejoice in Christ Jesus, and have no confidence in the flesh." (Philippians 3:3) For those who are intellectual, the accumulation of knowledge is very seductive. It gives a false sense of security, and is emotionally rewarding; the more knowledge that is accumulated, and the more prepared and equipped a person becomes, the more confident he is that he can handle life. This is a false belief, a false sense of security.

Knowledge can equip us, but cannot provide anything that the Spirit of God only provides (peace, joy, contentment...). Learning how the flesh fails us will not keep us from walking according to it; only dependence on God results in walking in the Spirit. Even the Word of God, which reveals the true condition of our heart, will not result in peace or joy unless we respond properly to that revelation. The only proper responses to God's Word are:

1. Humility: "'because your heart was tender, and you humbled yourself before God when you heard His words against this place and against its inhabitants, and you humbled yourself before Me, and you tore your clothes and wept before Me, I also have heard you,' says the LORD" (2 Chronicles 34:27);

2. Repentance: "Remember therefore how you have received and heard; hold fast and repent" (Revelation 3:3);

3. Obedience: "Do you not know that to whom you present yourselves slaves to obey, you are that one's slaves whom you obey, whether of sin leading to death, or of obedience leading to righteousness?" (Romans 6:16)

4. Reverence: "Likewise, exhort the young men to be sober-minded, in all things showing yourself to be a pattern of good works; in doctrine showing integrity, reverence, incorruptibility" (Titus 2:6-7);

5. Praise: "In God (I will praise His word), in God I have put my trust; I will not fear. What can flesh do to me?" (Psalm 56:4);

6. Trust: "So shall I have an answer for him who reproaches me, for I trust in Your word" (Psalm 119:42); and

7. Stand/hold fast: "...God from the beginning chose you for salvation through sanctification by the Spirit and belief in the truth, to which He called you by our gospel, for the obtaining of the glory of our Lord Jesus Christ. Therefore, brethren, stand fast and hold the traditions which you were taught, whether by word or our epistle" (2 Thessalonians 2: 13b-15); "Moreover, brethren, I declare to you the gospel which I preached to you, which also you received and

in which you stand, by which also you are saved, if you hold fast that word which I preached to you—unless you believed in vain" (1 Corinthians 15:1-2).

In summary, the accumulation of knowledge, arguments, analysis, rationalizations, strategies, or plans, will never accomplish what only dependence on God can. God's Word reveals the truth we need to know; if it does not benefit us, it is because we are not able to receive it (due to sin) or that we are not properly applying it. We cannot accomplish God's will in our own strength; natural strength cannot do that which is supernatural.

The flesh is comprised of emotions, desires, and intellect; to walk in the Spirit, we cannot rely on our fleshly strengths. Obedience and submission to God means denial of what the flesh demands. This sounds simple, but anyone who has denied the flesh knows that it means going against what we want physically, ignoring what we are feeling, and trusting God when it doesn't make any sense. That is why we often try to compromise with the flesh.

"It is a very evil choice for any soul under heaven to choose the least sin rather than the greatest affliction. Better to be under the greatest affliction than be under the guilt or power of any sin…"[13]

"And you know that He appeared in order to take away sins; no one who sins has seen Him or knows Him" (1 John 3:5).

– 1 John 3:5

"You adulteresses, do you not know that friendship with the world is hostility toward God? Therefore whoever wishes to be a friend of the world makes himself an enemy of God").

– James 4:4

Chapter 4
Compromising with the Flesh

od has no interest in fulfilling desires of the flesh. This may seem like a no-brainer, as the Scriptures admonish us to be characterized by the fruit of the Spirit, not of the flesh (Galatians 5). Yet do we live as if we really understand this?

I know that for years, I did not understand what this means. Whether I found myself in a situation of my choosing or not, I always wanted more, something better. Life was too boring, lonely, or difficult. Consequently, the majority of my time was spent trying to escape the reality I was faced with, either in a world of my own making (daydreams), or through books, movies, and so forth. This unhappiness was brought to God's attention on a regular basis, with sundry suggestions on how the situation could be remedied if He would do what I requested. What I misunderstood was what the blessings of God were.

I thought that if I served Him, behaved myself, that He would bless me. The Old Testament is replete with admonitions and promises from God that if Israel would follow and obey Him, they would be blessed. If they disobeyed and worshipped other idols, they would face the consequences (which they did over and over again). So I thought, life should be good for me; deprivation, loss, should not take place if I am following and obeying Him.

It does seem rather logical. But that is not what Christ told us to expect in the Gospels. He warned his disciples that they would face persecution, trials, and perhaps even death for His sake. "If they persecuted Me, they will also persecute you" (John 15:20). If we call ourselves by His name, we can expect to be treated as He was treated. Instead of telling them to expect tangible blessings, Jesus told them that a Comforter would come (John 14:16, 26). 1 Peter 1:6-7 and James 1:3-4 compliments Christ's teaching about trials by revealing that it is through trials that the fruit of the Spirit is developed.

The Christian walk in the New Testament emphasizes obedience that results in spiritual blessing; blessing in the Old Testament was physical in nature (land, no war or victory in war, food). There is a vital difference between New Testament believers and Old Testament believers. While salvation is basically the same (salvation through faith, i.e. Hebrews 11) New Testament believers have something Old Testament believers did not: the indwelling of the Holy Spirit. There are saints in the Old Testament who were filled with the Holy Spirit for certain occasions, but no permanent indwelling. Indwelling of the Spirit did not take place until Pentecost. Having an indwelling Spirit, believers in this day and age are to expect spiritual blessings. This isn't to say that God does not ever choose to bless us in tangible ways during the Church Age, but what it does mean is that the blessings we receive from obeying, trusting, and depending on God are first and foremost spiritual in nature.

Not understanding what God's blessings are (as the fruit of the Spirit) can lead to frustration for a Christian. Expectations are messed up. We end up angry, disappointed with a God who we think is not being very loving. We may even get to the point where we think, if this is Christianity, who wants it? By fixing our hopes on the tangible blessings down here (marriage, children, job, etc.) we miss out on the greatest blessing of all, which is the blessing that comes from experiencing God personally.

To live for the flesh and what it wants is to live for what is temporary, for what will pass away. Anything done in the flesh does not amount to

Why Am I So Miserable If This is the Lord's Will

anything; it does not have any value. What a waste it is to live for what the flesh desires!

Dying to the flesh is going to be painful. It is painful because the flesh always seeks activities that make life easier, more comfortable, more convenient and pleasurable, which is why compromising with the flesh becomes so tempting.

Compromising with the flesh, or rationalizing sin, has got to be the Achilles' heel that we all face. It is what the flesh wants us to do all the time — but there is no such thing as compromising with the flesh! To "compromise" is to choose the flesh and not the Spirit. But as we face trials and temptations, our fleshly nature wants to rationalize, and persuade us, to give in "just a little" so that it makes our life easier. The stronger the desire of the flesh is, the more convinced we can become that **we** need to take matters into **our** own hands. Whatever biblical standards we normally live by somehow fly right out the window, and we end up going our own way, and not God's. How, then, do we view and successfully overcome the trials and temptations that we face?

Trials

"It is good for me that I was afflicted, that I may learn Thy statutes" (Psalm 119:71).

"I know, O LORD, that Thy judgments are righteous, and that in faithfulness thou hast afflicted me" (Psalm 119:75).

Trials can be defined simply as trying circumstances in which there is either a loss, as in the loss of a loved one, occupation, health or possessions, or interpersonal conflict. The flesh's response to trying circumstances or people will be an effort to establish a sense of control, create a situation that is comfortable, or avoid that which is inconvenient. While severe trials are often what we recognize as tests of our faith, we will seek to compromise with the flesh the most in the way we respond to the everyday trials. Comfort, control, and convenience are what the flesh will seek on a daily basis, regardless of our circumstances.

For those who do not think they have control issues, think again. Everyone seeks to manifest control in an effort to obtain a sense of security and order, and to have their own way. Seeking to maintain order and have a sense of control in and of itself is not wrong; it is why and the extent to which control is sought that can be wrong. The right motivation for control is to do something God's way. When being in control is what we depend on to cope with life, rather than depending on God, that is sin.

Each person manifests a need for control in different areas and in different ways. While control is usually recognized in those who manipulate people into doing what they want, control can be seen in those who like to plan out any event in great detail as to avoid any possible disaster; it can be seen in those who are "neat freaks" who get stressed out if the house is not clean or in order; it can also be seen in the opposite, those who have to have clutter to find anything or to feel at home or secure. No one wants to be known as controlling, so we deceive ourselves; dependence on control not only is denied, it is also rationalized. This is self-righteousness, to rationalize sinful behavior and redefine what is right. To not depend on God is to make something or someone else our god. "For whoever shall keep the whole law, and yet stumble in one point, he is guilty of all." (James 2:10) When we choose to depend on our control mechanisms, we demonstrate a lack of acknowledgement and faith in the sovereignty of God; we rebel in doing things His way and in His timing; we make ourselves the standard for truth and conduct; and we do not trust His provision or care. "Trust in the Lord

Why Am I So Miserable If This is the Lord's Will

with all your heart and lean not unto your own understanding; in all your ways acknowledge Him, and He shall direct your paths" (Proverbs 3:5-6).

As with any stronghold of the flesh, a sense of control can be achieved, albeit temporarily; but it is never complete and must always be pursued. Any and every effort to manage, control, or make better by any means of the flesh is for naught. Any sense of control over circumstances or people is an illusion; when God is already in control, we cannot be. We only fool ourselves if we think that any success can be achieved through our attempts to control. Even if we are not seeking to control others, any attempt to control anything else is evidence that we are not submitting our will to God, and that we do not trust Him to take care of us the way we think He ought to.

How then, do we not give into the flesh's demands for control? We need to rest in the knowledge that God is in control; that He will work everything out according to His good will and purpose. It is waiting patiently and joyfully for His will to be revealed and accomplished, knowing that He will do it! Remember that "God has not given us a spirit of fear, but of power and of love and of a sound mind" (2 Timothy 1:7). To seek to be in control and not trust God is to let fear be the master of us. It can be fear of: 1) pain, injury to ourselves or others; 2) the opinion of others or failure; or 3) not getting what we want or need when we want it. Regardless of whatever the reason, the only way to "handle it" is to trust that no matter what happens, God is in control and will enable us to get through it with joy, peace, contentment, satisfaction, and hope, and especially with the love of God.

In addition to control, we also pursue comfort and convenience rather than accepting God's way. I like to think that I am a pretty tough person and that I can do without a lot; but if I am honest, if we are all honest, there are certain things we insist on to ensure a comfortable life, and one as stress-free as possible. Pain is a thing so abhorred that even minor inconveniences are treated as though they were a personal attack. We have to have our coffee, chocolate, rest, or alcohol or our social life, parties, fun, or anything else that makes us feel good. Comfort becomes our god when doing what feels good becomes the rule by which we live our life. "Therefore, whether you eat or drink, or whatever you do, do all to the glory of God" (1 Corinthians 10:31). We cannot serve the flesh's desire for comfort and do it all to the glory of God at the same time. Doing what glorifies God may mean doing that which is outside our comfort zone.

While comfort has to do mainly with our environment, our activities and our appetite, inconvenience has to do with how we respond to the demands that other people place on us. It is avoiding what we don't want to do and anything that requires any effort or sacrifice on our part. Inconvenience becomes our god when we make our personal happiness of more importance than anyone else's, including God's. Clearly this contradicts the command to "Love God... and thy neighbor" (Luke 10:27).

It isn't that we cannot achieve a sense of control, comfort and convenience in our lives through our own efforts; it is that we can **never** achieve the sense of arrival, the point at which we no longer have to strive to have control, comfort, and convenience. No matter how long we pursue these three, it will never bring the peace, healing and strength that we crave during times of trial. On the contrary, the more we pursue an avoidance of pain it never really is avoided, only anesthetized. Only God can give genuine comfort and healing. The flesh can only cover up pain; it never provides anything which actually deals with it, and as a result only prolongs the pain we are in. But pain has a way of driving us to seek immediate relief through fleshly means, which will always be seen in our attempt to figure out what we have to do to get what we want. "Select the B you desire, then perform the A that leads to it. There's an A—a strategy—that leads to every B—a goal. That's the law of linearity."[14] This law of linearity is a very natural and logical approach to life; it is what makes the most sense to us. It seems to work, and would if what the flesh desired actually met our need; since it doesn't, we end up in

Why Am I So Miserable If This is the Lord's Will

an endless pursuit of something that feels good, but doesn't do us any good. This is a continual burden which places pressure on us, sapping our energies and strength. Our flesh will always fail us; God never fails. "My flesh and my heart fail; but God is the strength of my heart and my portion forever" (Psalm 73:26).

Isn't it interesting that the more we try to protect ourselves, the more we isolate and burden ourselves?! When we make avoidance of pain or discomfort our goal, it is never achieved to our satisfaction. We become trapped in the continual struggle of self-protection. Fear of encountering something too painful, too stressful rules our lives. What is the solution to this fear? Self-protection only isolates us from life, and does not remove the fear. The only way to fight fear is with the spirit of love and power, and the sound mind that God has given us. (2 Timothy 2:17). By God's grace and power, we can choose not to be ruled by fear, but by love.

Pain is seen as the problem, instead of discovering what the problem actually is and dealing with it. Without pain, problems and injuries would either go unnoticed or would be ignored. Pain points to a need; instead of it being something to be avoided or simply endured, it needs to be seen for the call to attention that it is. Unfortunately, instead of addressing the problem that the pain is revealing, we seek to medicate, alleviate and obliterate the pain; when the pain is temporarily relieved, we think "problem solved!" This, of course, does not take care of the problem at all.

But what about painful situations in which we are truly not at fault? What about suffering when we have not done anything wrong, and we cannot see how it is suffering in Christ's name (being persecuted because we are Christians)? Or, being stuck in a painful situation about which we already have done everything that we know to do biblically, and yet it is not resolved? What is pain calling attention to here, or what possible good reason could there be for it?

The Apostle Paul was faced with a trial that he could not understand; 2 Corinthians 12:7-9 describes how he sought the Lord three times for it to be removed, but it wasn't. God responded to him saying: "My grace is sufficient for you, for My strength is made perfect in weakness." (v.9) To depend on God, live in obedience to His Word, trust and believe in Him is to walk by faith and by the Spirit. Trials are a testing of our faith: "that the genuineness of your faith…may be found to praise, honor and glory at the revelation of Jesus Christ" (1 Peter 1:7). The more uncomfortable and painful a situation becomes, the more inclined we are to question God's goodness and love for us. But whether a trial is as small as a minor inconvenience or as severe as a loss of a family member, how we respond to our circumstances will demonstrate whether we believe that what God said is true, that He is good, and that He will take care of us.

When we are going through a time of trial, being sure of our faith in God is essential. Without being sure of our salvation and faith in God, we can be led to believe that He has abandoned us when He has not, or that everything we have been taught about Him from His Word is a sham. It may be that because of a trial that we are going through or have gone through, that questions and issues arise such as: "Am I really saved?;" "Can God really be good?;" "Is my relationship with God what it should be?"

I recently received a letter from a friend who was struggling with such questions. A question she asked me was: "How can I be sure that I have faith?" This is my reply to her:

As to whether your faith is strong or not or whether you have a personal relationship with God or not, the answers to that are also found in the Word of God. First, how is faith measured or determined? Hebrews 11:1 defines faith as "the substance of things hoped for, the evidence of things not seen." The rest of the chapter gives examples of people who had faith: Abel, Enoch, Abraham, and so forth. What did these people have in common? God either commanded them to do something and they did it, even though the rightness of that choice was not evident at the time; or, they believed what God had said, and lived according to it. This is faith – believing what God has said is true, and acting according to it, even if you cannot see how it is true at the moment. What better example of something that requires faith than believing that God says that Jesus died on the cross for our sins, and that if we will believe on Him, that we will have eternal life? We cannot see God; we cannot see heaven. Believing that both exist requires faith. But I would also add that not believing in God, and believing that this world existed millions of years (which is based on the interpretation of evidence, not on solid proof) also requires faith. Faith is something that is exercised whether you are a Christian or not. It is trusting in something to be true even though it has not been fully proven. I cannot speak for anyone else, but I would much rather place my faith and trust in God than in anyone or anything else.

How do we know we have faith or that it is strong enough? Well, the first way to measure that is to determine what we really believe and, second, to look at how we live. How we believe determines how we live. Do we want to honor God? Do we seek to please Him? Do we repent of our sin? Do we seek to obey His Word? Do we seek to love Him and others? Most importantly, do we do good works out of love for Him or to try to earn His approval? What we do should not be out of guilt or manipulation, or determination to earn favor or approval. It should be out of a desire to please Him because we love Him.

What if we don't feel love for Him? Feelings come and go. If we lack love or faith, all we need to do is ask God for it. God wants us to know His love for us, and wants us to love in return. Remember also that love isn't just what we feel for another person, it is doing what is right and good for another person, regardless of whether we feel like it at the moment or not.

Faith is measured by the degree to which we believe in and subsequently act upon something. Faith in God, then, is to believe what He has told us in His Word and to live in obedience to it, even if it doesn't seem to make sense. There are things that are going to happen that we will never understand why until we get to heaven. Faith is believing that God is good despite the evil we see going on around us, and that He is in control and that He will take care of us and has a plan for us and for the world. We know that we cannot see things the way that God does; we also know we cannot see or understand all that happens or why it does. Only God does.

Those that have little faith are those that require a sign, or proof from God that He is real or that what He has said is true. In the Sermon on the Mount, Jesus chided those with little faith. How was that lack of faith exemplified? Worry. Jesus said, "Therefore do not worry, saying, 'What shall we eat?' or 'What shall we drink?' or 'What shall we wear?' For after all these things the Gentiles seek. For your heavenly Father knows that you need all these things. But seek first the kingdom of God and His righteousness, and all these things shall be added to you"(Matthew 6: 31-33). Worry is a lack of faith. It demonstrates a lack of belief that God is going to take care of us.

We all have at some point in our lives worried about something. Don't think that just because we do, that we aren't showing ourselves to be true followers of God, and therefore might not go to heaven. In John Piper's book *Future Grace*, he describes true followers of God by how they respond to sin. He comments on Psalm 25:

In other words, even though we sin every day in various ways, there is a profound difference between sinners who keep God's covenant (v.10) and sinners who don't. The issue facing us in light of this

Why Am I So Miserable If This is the Lord's Will

psalm is whether we "wait for the Lord" (v.21) and "take refuge in Him"(v.20) and "fear" Him (v.12) and are "humble" before Him (v.9) and, in this way, "keep His covenant" (v.10).[15]

How we respond to sin will indicate whether we are followers of God or not. Do we try to pay for it ourselves, cover it up, or deny it? Or do we humble ourselves before God, and receive His mercy and grace? If we feel our faith is not strong, we need to ask God to increase our faith.

If all that pain ever does is cause us to depend more upon God, walk closer to Him, cause us to become sure of our salvation and increase our faith, it is well worth it. Those who have intense emotional pain may find this difficult to accept. When in a lot of pain all we want is for it to end; we cannot see any justifiable good to it whatsoever. This is the ultimate test of faith: to trust that God is good and that He loves us, despite the pain He is allowing in our life. It is to believe in what we cannot see or feel at the time. This is only possible by the grace and power of God. "If any of you lacks wisdom, let him ask of God, who gives to all liberally and without reproach, and it will be given to him. But let him ask in faith, with no doubting..." (James 1:5-6).

Pain is not the enemy. **Sin** is the enemy; it is what ultimately makes us miserable, not our circumstances. "Sin" may be a term with bad connotations for those who have been brow-beaten or made to feel condemned when they have repented of sin, or for those who think sin only applies to behavior that is blatantly or extremely wrong. Sin is simply any attitude, word or action that is done according to our own way or will rather than God's. If sin is not considered enemy No. 1, something else will be. That something else will be pain in one form or another: 1) a loss of control, comfort, or convenience, 2) loss of friends/family, job, home, etc. and 3) injury, whether physical, mental, or emotional. Sin, while it is enjoyable at the moment (and can either dulls or distracts us from pain), blocks our fellowship with God and what He provides. Pain, which is not enjoyable at the moment, may serve to draw us closer to Him.

Even if we recognize that sin really is our enemy, it is deeply engrained in our flesh to avoid whatever causes it discomfort, stress, or pain. When we hate pain more than we hate sin, we serve ourselves before we serve God; in other words, protecting ourselves has priority over serving, loving, trusting, and obeying God. Protecting ourselves may enable us to avoid pain, but it will also keep us from depending on the Lord.

When pain is the enemy, not only do we avoid it for ourselves personally (directly), but we seek to keep others from it as well. This is especially true for those who have empathy for the pain that other people are feeling. It is understandable to not want to see one of our loved ones hurt. But when sin is seen as causing greater damage that pain ever could, instead of viewing all pain as bad, we will help them discover the source of the pain and then to depend on God for the healing, strength and comfort that is needed. Are they learning something vital, are they growing in Christ as a result of what they are going through? As much as we do not want to see loved ones hurt, pain is to be accepted while depending on God's comfort and grace, knowing that God will only ever allow that which is for our ultimate good.

We can live (and even live well) with pain with God's help; we cannot truly live without God. Not only can we have God's strength to get through pain, there is comfort and hope knowing that any pain that God allows is for a good purpose (even if we cannot see it at the time). James tells us that "the testing of your faith produces patience. But let patience have its perfect work, that you may be perfect and complete, lacking nothing" (James 1:3b-4). This is echoed in the teaching of Jesus who tells us that "every branch that bears fruit, He prunes it, that it may bear more fruit" (John 15:2b).

Afflictions or trials are opportunities to be emptied of self and filled with God's life. "For we who live are constantly being delivered over to death for Jesus' sake that the life of Jesus may be manifested in our mortal flesh" (2 Corinthians 4:11). The theme of self-death in Scripture continues: "Most assuredly, I say to you, unless a grain of wheat falls into the ground and dies, it remains alone; but if it dies, it produces much grain" (John 12:24-25).

To stop avoiding pain, when it is has been a lifelong habit, can only be done by relying on and trusting God. Stop seeking relief from emotional pain by avoiding, or trying to avoid (escape) what God has allowed! Relief can only be found in acceptance of His will, trust in His goodness, and reliance on His strength and comfort. When we place our confidence in God no matter what pain comes our way, we will be able to not only get through the pain with joy, but will also "bear much fruit" in ways we had not anticipated.

It is clear that the flesh places a priority on avoidance of pain. Even if conscious thought is not there, the flesh gives priority to our protection (safety from harm), comfort (pleasures) and self-preservation. It does not trust God to protect, care, or provide. This is why we are tempted to try and compromise with the flesh: we want what it offers.

Temptation

Temptation always has to do with what this world offers: "For all that is in the world—the lust of the flesh, the lust of the eyes, and the pride of life—is not of the Father but is of the world" (1 John 2:16). "But each one is tempted when he is drawn away by his own desires and enticed" (James 1:14). Note that the desires mentioned in James are described in 1 John.

Temptation is that which lures us to act independently of God. Depending on what we are being tempted to do, this may or may not be readily apparent; most of the time it isn't. Temptations to sin are not simply to just have enjoyment; they are an enticement to worship, or to serve someone or something else other than God. Temptation always states a lie as a fact; that what God provides or allows is insufficient, unfair, not good or not enough. It tells us that it will satisfy us more than God can or will. Those who love God do not want to sin; but at the end of the day, we have always sinned in one way or another. Why do we do this? It is because the activity presented to us will not look like something that can damage our relationship with God. There are times when it is quite clear that what is appealing to us at the moment is wrong and would be offensive to God. But where temptation trips us up the most is when the activity is easy to rationalize. We usually do not start out our days thinking, "I want to sin today." We do not want to sin. We just want to have fun. It isn't so much that we don't want to walk in the Spirit, as much as it is that we don't want to give up what the flesh desires.

How does temptation tempt? It promises freedom from boredom, pain, or discomfort without any or very little consequences. There are two rationales at work here: 1) that whatever action is being suggested is harmless—"it won't hurt anyone;" and 2) that whatever we are being tempted to do or have is better than what God is providing and can provide for us. Temptation lures us away from God by causing us to doubt: the veracity of His Word, His law, His statutes, and the consequences of not keeping it; and the goodness of God (how can a good God allow pain?).

We sin because we have a misunderstanding of what God's love is and what goodness is. When pain is considered the worst evil to be avoided, love is defined by keeping the one we love from being hurt or experiencing pain at all times. When pain is considered evil and God allows painful things to happen, his love and goodness are then in question. That is the problem: pain is not evil; **sin is evil**. If we don't understand this we will feel let down and deserted by God when pain comes into our lives. When we don't get the escape and relief from pain that we want, we will seek it elsewhere. Doubting God's Word and His goodness is exactly how Satan lured Eve away from God: "Now the serpent was more cunning than any beast of the field which

Why Am I So Miserable If This is the Lord's Will

the LORD God had made. And he said to the woman, "Has God indeed said, 'You shall not eat of every tree of the garden?'"(Genesis 3:1).

When we sin, even if we did not consciously seek to rebel against God, that is what our actions accomplish. To give into temptation and sin is to reject God and His will. Choosing to sin means that we do not believe what God said about the consequences of sin, or that we do not care.

Temptation to sin will be the strongest when we are unhappy or in very difficult circumstances. We don't like waiting for His timing and whatever we are stuck with. When we are in pain, anything to alleviate it is very appealing. We will gladly put up with whatever consequences if the pain will just go away. But anyone who has ever sinned to alleviate pain knows that while it may give brief, temporary relief, the root of the problem is still there and the pain just comes right back.

Being tempted is not sinning; **yielding** to temptation is sin. "But each one is tempted when he is drawn away by his own desires and enticed. Then, when desire has conceived, it gives birth to sin; and sin, when it is full-grown, brings forth death." (James 1:14-15). "Walk in the Spirit, and you shall not fulfill the lust of the flesh" (Galatians 5:16). The only way to deal with our desires (strong or otherwise) is to walk in the Spirit. There's no other way. We cannot think our way out of a temptation. The human mind has the amazing capacity for rationalization. We can easily start out with the intention of not giving in, and end up sinning because we managed to find a way to make it alright. The only way to deal with temptation is to turn from it to God. "Therefore submit to God. Resist the devil and he will flee from you" (James 4:7).

The very fact that rationalization results in an outward action of sin is revealing—we sin first in our minds before it is acted out. Sin is not simply what we say and do; it is what we choose to see and listen to, and what we choose to think about. It is not an unbidden thought that comes to mind; it is what we choose to dwell on. We tend to concern ourselves the most with sins of word and deed, and not that of thought. Yet, "as he thinks in his heart, so is he" (Prov. 23:7).

When we choose to dwell on whatever is true, honorable, right, pure, lovely, of good repute (Philippians 4:8), we choose not to dwell on all other things. The Apostle Paul emphasizes the importance of battling temptations and the flesh in our thoughts in Romans 12:2: "And do not be conformed to this world, but be transformed by the renewing of your mind, that you may prove what is that good and acceptable and perfect will of God" (see also 2 Corinthians 10:5).

Since what we see and listen to, as well as what we say and do can be sin, how do we evaluate what we watch, read, and listen to? Philippians 4:8 works here as well. We have to ask: Does it cause us to think about that which isn't good, true, and so forth? Does it draw us closer to God or draw us away from Him? Does it appeal to our fleshly desires, or does it support our spiritual walk with Christ, with His Spirit? Do we try to justify what we do? In other words, what are our motives?

What we say and do is a result of our motives. If our motives are rooted in fleshly desires, any change we attempt to make in our behavior will only give us the appearance of having changed; no real change will take place because we are still acting according to our flesh. God is the only one who makes real change possible. Only through knowing Him can our motives change. If instead of being motivated by fleshly desires, we are motivated by the love of God, the resulting change in our behavior is real. Because of God's great love, we have become a new creation (2 Corinthians 5:17); we have come out of the darkness and into "His marvelous light." (1 Peter 2:9) "Beloved, now we are children of God…" (1 John 3:2). Those who are His children love Him (1 John 4:19) and want to deny the flesh and submit to God. But even if this is our desire, if we try to change without relying on and submitting to the Spirit, we are being motivated by fleshly desires. Any change motivated and fueled by the flesh will fail when the rewards that the flesh was getting are taken away, or something more rewarding comes along. This is how trials and temptations reveal who and what we are serving. Those who are His children will realize their wrong motives and repent; those who are not children of God will not blame themselves for their lack of faith or change in behavior but will blame God or Christianity and end up rejecting both. This is why there are so many that "depart from the faith" when persecution comes. Those who "depart" never were children of God in the first place; they were saying the right things, doing what was right in the eyes of men, but were not living in dependence and submission to God.

What we are motivated by, what we rely on, what we are trying to accomplish will all reveal to us whether we are walking according to the flesh or walking according to the Spirit. Are the decisions we make based on what we want, or on what God wants? To answer these questions often means giving up something the flesh doesn't want to give up! Yet Paul exhorts us: "You have not yet resisted to bloodshed, striving against sin" (Hebrews 12:4).

These questions lead to the heart of the matter: our attitude toward sin. This will be apparent by what we tolerate—whether we fudge standards to make them easier to live by, or continually seek godliness and holiness. Our attitude toward sin is revealed by how sensitive we are to the smallest infraction and by how uncomfortable we are with it. Our aim needs to be to despise sin more than anything else: more than discomfort, pain, inconvenience, boredom, or whatever we avoid more than sin. We need to see sin through God's eyes. Complaining, worrying, self-centeredness, gossip and gluttony are just as wrong as rape, murder, or theft. Why? Because all sin separates us and destroys our relationship with God. Since knowing and enjoying God is infinitely better than anything else, why settle for less? God's way is always better than our way, even though giving up our way requires sacrifice.

Praise God that we do not have to be stuck in the meaningless pursuit of pleasure. Though temptations can be powerful, God always provides a way of avoiding them or escaping them: "No temptation has overtaken you except such as is common to man; but God is faithful, who will not allow you to be tempted beyond what you are able, but with the temptation will also make the way of escape, that you may be able to bear it" (1 Corinthians 10:13). Many temptations can be avoided simply by not going to places where we will be tempted, and by not watching, reading, or listening to what we know will either provide opportunity to be tempted or will definitely lead to temptation. Scripture advises us to flee fornication (1 Corinthians 6:18), flee from idolatry (1 Corinthians 10:14), flee from the love of money (1 Timothy 6:10-12), and flee youthful lusts (2 Timothy 2:22). Fleeing these things is to simply not go where we are going to be tempted, and to not look at anything that is going to tempt us. We also have the full armor of God at our disposal (Ephesians 6:10-18).

Salvation, truth, righteousness, the Word of God, faith, peace, and prayer can enable us to stand firm against temptation and trial. Christ, when tempted, responded to each temptation with the Word of God (Luke 4:1-13). Nowhere in Scripture is there an example or command to fight temptation with intellect, emotion, or will. Whenever we think we can handle temptation, when we place confidence in ourselves, we will fail. Simply knowing the right thing to do does not guarantee victory! We must place our confidence in the Lord and in His Word; to place it in our intellect, or in what we can see, feel or do is to fail before we even begin.

Temptation never fully delivers what it promises. We may find that we are continually disappointed because either our flesh or Satan has given us false and unrealistic expectations. It is amazing that even if nothing is ever what we quite hoped it would be, we don't give up on the pursuit of pleasure. Anytime we serve the flesh, we end up on a treadmill, running nowhere, getting nowhere—always striving, hoping for something that satisfies, but never finding it. It is a depressing way to live. "Do you not know that to whom you present yourselves slaves to obey, you are that one's slaves whom you obey, whether of sin leading to death, or of obedience leading to righteousness?" (Romans 6:16) Is any pleasure of the flesh worth the damage it does to your relationship with God?

Though the solution is simple, it is not easy! Especially when our desires are strong and the flesh demands to have what it wants! Don't op-out for the quick, easy, feels-good-but-does-no-good solution that the flesh offers! Go for that which may not be what we think we want to do at the moment, but for that which we will never regret doing in the end: God's will. His will is always accomplished when we seek to honor Him by doing what He says, and by loving Him and loving others. When we don't "feel" like it, we need to pray not only that we won't give in to the temptation, but also, that we will even want to pray. Be honest with God. It will not shock Him. Be respectful and humble, recognizing sin and inability; ask for His help to trust Him and increase faith. A lack of faith or belief in what God has said or that He will provide is always the cause of sin.

When we do yield to temptation we will experience: 1) consequence of that particular sin (Romans 6:23); 2) loss of fellowship with God and others, which results in the loss of peace, joy, and contentment (Psalm 66:18, Proverbs 18: 19); and 3) loss of spiritual discernment (1 Corinthians 2:14). It is true that for each believer our sins are covered by the blood of Christ; God sees us as righteous (Romans 4:6-8). Jesus took upon himself our condemnation (1 John 2:2). We do not have to face condemnation, but to choose the flesh keeps us from all that God has for us.

We can expect resistance from our flesh when we seek to walk in the Spirit. The flesh will not give up quietly. The flesh, just like Satan, **lies**. It will convince us that we "need" more sleep, more food, sex outside of marriage, etc. But giving up these activities means giving up instant gratification; it means trusting God to take care of us when we feel physically or emotionally stressed and want immediate relief. The flesh will try to convince us that the only solution is the solution it presents. To give up what we are sure is the only thing that is going to make us feel better seems pointless, suffering for nothing. The irony is when we do give it up and spend time with God, we find we didn't need it after all; we are better off without it. When we allow our feelings to dictate our actions, they are never satisfied; but, when we act on what is right, our feelings will follow. We will find that it is not a "drag" to lead a holy life, but a "blast" (in a spiritual sense). Walking in the Spirit blows away living life any other way.

If choosing God and His way is so much better than living life according to the flesh, it then follows that those who walk in the Spirit do not put any confidence in the flesh. The Apostle Paul describes true believers as those who "have no confidence in the flesh" (Philippians 3:3). We may be quick to deny that we put any confidence in the flesh, but the flesh has a way of appearing to have good intentions, masquerading as righteousness. The Psalmist says "see if there is any wicked way in me" (Psalm 139:24). The religious leaders in Israel at the time of Christ (the Pharisees and the Sadducees) whom Christ called "whitewashed tombs" are an example of confidence in the flesh (Matthew 23:27). The religious leaders were very zealous at keeping the law and even added hundreds of laws to it; but their intent was to promote themselves and gain the approval of men, not of God (Matthew 23). Theirs was self-righteousness, not a righteousness that comes from faith. "For the promise ...was not to Abraham, or to his seed through the Law, but through the righteousness of faith" (Romans 4:13). The Pharisees and religious leaders looked very devoted to God; but God knew the intention of their hearts, that it was evil (Luke 11:39; Matthew 16:1-6). An action may be "good" in the sense that the action performed benefits someone else; but if that action is not born out of a love for God and others, then it is an action born out of selfish motives and desires.

For each of us, the way in which we tend to rely on the flesh will be different. For me, it is the desire to understand why. I felt that if I could understand why and how something happened, I could get a handle on it and could deal with it. This can be achieved with a measure of success; but as with all means of the flesh, it ultimately fails. Knowing why will relieve our mind, but it doesn't keep us from giving into temptation and sinning. Other people seek emotional resolution. But no matter how we rely on the flesh or try to relieve stress or solve problems in the flesh, it never will get to the root of the problem. The reality we are left with is that as much as we try to protect ourselves, not only do we fail to do so we also alienate other people in the process.

Worse than this is the alienation from God that results when we attempt to deal with the problems and temptations of life in our own strength. The Apostle Paul illustrates the gravity of this: "I also count all things loss for the excellence of the knowledge of Christ Jesus my Lord..." (Philippians 3:8). To choose to rely on ourselves, on what we can know, or on what we can feel, rather than placing our faith and trust in God and in the Lord Jesus Christ, is to lose out on knowing God.

If we think that it is impossible to deny the flesh all the time, it is. It is impossible to defeat the flesh with any fleshly strength. But denying the flesh and walking in the Spirit is possible with God's strength. In Romans 6, Paul tells us that we have been freed from the bondage to sin, and are now slaves to righteousness (v.18). God has made it possible to choose whom or what we obey: sin or God. We are to consider ourselves "to be dead indeed to sin, but alive to God in Christ Jesus our Lord" (v.11). Walking in the Spirit is only possible with the Spirit's help; but it will not happen simply because we want it to, nor will it happen automatically. Paul continues in this chapter to exhort them (v.12,13, 16, 19b):

> *"Therefore do not let sin reign in your mortal body that you should obey it in its lusts. And do not present your members as instruments of unrighteousness to sin, but present yourselves to God as being alive*

from the dead, and your members as instruments of righteousness to God...Do you not know that to whom you present yourselves as slaves to obey, you are that one's slaves whom you obey, whether of sin leading to death, or of obedience leading to righteousness? ...So now present your members as slaves of righteousness for holiness."

We do not walk in the Spirit when we are obeying the dictates of the flesh, or following a system of rules or traditions; it is about choosing to submit to God's will every day, in everything we think, say, and do, all for His glory. Trying to do His will our way is not doing His will. Doing God's will, then, is comprehensive and all-encompassing; we cannot do it part-way. We either do it His way or not at all.

Remember that we are not alone in this struggle against sin and the flesh. "If God is for us, who can be against us?" (Romans 8:31) God has also provided spiritual brothers and sisters in Christ who can encourage us in the struggles we are having. We need to have someone we can trust, who we can be accountable to — not to condemn, but to exhort and encourage us in our spiritual walk. Confrontation is simply talking to other believers about sinful behavior. Condemnation does not offer a solution but rejects the sinner as well as the sin. We need to make sin the enemy—not the sinner. Confrontation of sin is a vital part of being accountable to one another. The person we want to be accountable to is one who is willing to confront us when they see sin our lives. It isn't simply a matter of saying, "Hang in there!" but finding out what sin issues need to be addressed and bringing those matters to the Lord together. "Confess your trespasses to one another, and pray for one another, that you may be healed" (James 5:16). How do we encourage one another in the struggle against sin? By directing each other to restore our relationship with God. Our relationship with God is restored when we repent of our sin and seek to love Him with our whole being. He is ready and willing to receive all who will confess their sin, no matter what it is, and turn from it to Him (1 John 1:9).

Tolerance

"But these, like natural brute beasts made to be caught and destroyed, speak evil of the things they do not understand, and will utterly perish in their own corruption, and will receive the wages of unrighteousness, as those who count it pleasure to carouse in the daytime. They are spots and blemishes, carousing in their own deceptions while they feast with you" (2 Peter 2:12-13).

A false teaching that is prevalent today is tolerance, which is being embraced by Christians individually and by many denominations and local churches. This false teaching is a distortion of what the Bible teaches us about love and how it is applied, and about how sin is defined and treated.

Tolerance, as it is practiced today, means not showing disapproval or rejection of another person based on race, color, social standing, disability, religion, or work/school performance. Increasingly, this is becoming as stringent as to inhibit the free exercise of speech and religion. To say anything that is considered by another to be offensive is not allowed; activities are prevented even at the potential for offense. But while tolerance of differences is the rule, tolerance is not extended to those who are considered intolerant, or to whose views are considered intolerant. The result: though tolerance would imply that discrimination is a thing of the past, it instead legitimizes what it considers to be the only acceptable form of discrimination—discrimination toward anyone who believes that there is an absolute standard for truth, especially toward those who hold that the Bible is that standard.

What are the results of our current culture of tolerance? Children are not held to high expectations (no one is allowed to feel bad for not achieving the highest grade). Team learning is encouraged, with the result that the weakest link is carried by the rest, rather than being challenged to improve. Workers are allowed to get by with mediocre work and service. At all levels of society, people are not being held accountable for their behavior. Instead of being allowed to experience consequences, people are felt sorry for and the natural consequences of their actions are alleviated or even eliminated.

Tolerance is practiced in the church when walking according to the flesh is allowed and even approved. "Minor" sins are overlooked; enjoying oneself, being happy is given more priority than being holy and loving God. Happiness is defined not by knowing God and experiencing Him, but by feeling good. This is idolatry. Tolerance in the church also means that accountability is not practiced; people are not held to the standards in God's Word. A church becomes a social club, rather than a body of believers who are in the process of being conformed to the image of Christ. This is in contrast to what God teaches us about being accountable to one another, as expressed in James 5:16, where we are commanded to confess our sins to one another.

One of the main reasons that tolerance is practiced in the church is due to a misunderstanding of love, believing that loving someone is about keeping them from all emotional and physical pain. Love, when properly understood and practiced, sees that pain is a natural process of growth and learning, and is necessary. Love, as exemplified in God's Word, is not what **feels** good to them and to us; it is doing what **is** good. It is true that love is not rude and is kind, but it is also true that it "does not rejoice in iniquity, but rejoices in the truth." (1 Corinthians 13:4-6). To create a pain-free life for someone is like allowing a drug addict to continue taking drugs (slowly killing themselves in the process) just so that they can experience all the pleasure they want. Dealing with sin, and any reliance on the flesh is painful; but without the pain of self-denial, confession and repentance, there cannot be the benefit of walking in the Spirit.

Why Am I So Miserable If This is the Lord's Will

A church that practices tolerance not only lacks true love, it is lacking in faith. Faith is belief in action; it is being willing to do what God tells us to do, even if we do not understand, or if it will be painful. Instead of trying to live life on God's terms, a person or church that practices tolerance lives life on their terms—an "it's good for me" relativistic approach to Christianity. This contradicts God's command in Proverbs 3:5, in which we are told to "trust in the Lord with all your heart and lean not on your own understanding."

All that we need to be delivered from self and sin is to be willing to see it, to call it by its right name, to brand it with its true character, to pass sentence of death upon it, to give God the right to slay it and to stand upon the sentence without compromise. There is power enough in the sword of the Spirit, in the blood of Calvary, in the faithfulness, love and grace of God to make us dead indeed to sin but alive to God through Jesus Christ our Lord![16]

For the practice of tolerance to be eliminated, we must die to self. To die to self means no more "I"—I want this, I don't want that, I don't feel like doing it, I won't, I don't like this, I will, etc. It is to no longer concern ourselves with what we want to do, but with what God wants us to do. "I have been crucified with Christ; it is no longer I who live, but Christ lives in me; and the life which I now live in the flesh I live by faith in the Son of God, who loved me and gave Himself for me" (Galatians 2:20). "For if you live according to the flesh you will die; but if by the Spirit you put to death the deeds of the body, you will live" (Romans 8:13).

"He who observes the day, observes it to the Lord; and he who does not observe the day, to the Lord he does not observe it. He who eats, eats to the Lord, for he gives God thanks; and he who does not eat, to the Lord he does not eat, and gives God thanks. For none of us lives to himself, and no one dies to himself. For if we live, we live to the Lord; and if we die, we die to the Lord. Therefore, whether we live or die, we are the Lord's" (Romans 14:6-8).

"...and He died for all, that those who live should live no longer for themselves, but for Him who died for them and rose again" (2 Corinthians 5:15).

Tolerance as it is practiced by the world and by Christians has been around for a long time: doing what we are comfortable doing, not being accountable for what we do, and doing away with any standard or belief that would hold us accountable. Ever since the Fall, this has been the desire of the flesh. Although we may never intend to go against what God has given us in His Word, we can end up doing that very thing if we become tolerant of that which falls short of the glory of God. Our flesh and Satan both would like to have us do only that which feels good and will try to convince us that not doing things God's way is alright by mixing truth with lies; in the end, we are led astray. That is why our constant need is to remember what truth is by meditating on God's Word.

Tolerance, which is so popular today, is a serious attack on each person's relationship with God and others, and to the Church as a whole. We need to be on guard against it, for it compromises with the flesh. We cannot compromise what we believe or the standards of God's Word without destroying our relationship with Him and with others. There is no compromising with the flesh! We either yield to God or to our flesh. Compromise requires rejection of God's Word, His way, or His standards. Tolerance practiced in such a way will result in a break in fellowship with the Father and dysfunctional relationships with everyone else! So the question is: will we be tolerant of sin? Will we reject God's standards for our own? Are the world's standards more important than God's standards? If the answer for any of these questions is yes, then we have just chosen to turn from God.

Why Am I So Miserable If This is the Lord's Will

"I bless thee that great sin draws out great grace, that, although the least sin deserves infinite punishment because done against an infinite God, yet there is mercy for me..."[17]

"Abide in Me, and I in you. As the branch cannot bear fruit of itself, unless it abides in the vine, neither can you, unless you abide in Me. I am the vine, you are the branches. He who abides in Me, and I in him, bears much fruit; for without Me you can do nothing...As the Father loved Me, also have loved you; abide in My love".

– John 15:4-5, 9a

Chapter 5
The Flesh & Our Relationship with God

*T*he breakdown in our relationship with God resulted in the formation of our sinful, fleshly nature. In Genesis 3 we find out why there is a constant resistance to God and His ways, why we are burdened with a fleshly nature bent on self-destruction. This was never God's desire for us. God created us to find fulfillment in Him and to give Him glory. David testifies in Psalm 16:11: "You will show me the path of life; in Your presence is fullness of joy." We are admonished to do all to the glory of God (1 Corinthians 10:31). It is recorded in Genesis that we are God's creation: "God created man in His own image…God saw everything that He had made, and indeed it was very good" (Genesis 1:27, 31).

But all that was good in creation was ruined when Adam and Eve disobeyed God. Though we were created by God, for God, man's sin separated him from God and blocked fellowship and relationship with Him when he asserted his independence from God in eating from the tree of knowledge of good and evil, as recorded in Genesis 3: 1-13:

> *"Now the serpent was more cunning than any beast of the field which the LORD God had made. And he said to the woman, 'Has God indeed said, "You shall not eat of*

every tree of the garden"?' And the woman said to the serpent, 'We may eat the fruit of the trees of the garden; but of the fruit of the tree which is in the midst of the garden, God has said, "You shall not eat it, nor shall you touch it, lest you die."' Then the serpent said to the woman, 'You will not surely die. For God knows that in the day you eat of it your eyes will be opened, and you will be like God, knowing good and evil.' So when the woman saw that the tree was good for food, that it was pleasant to the eyes, and a tree desirable to make one wise, she took of its fruit and ate. She also gave to her husband with her, and he ate. Then the eyes of both of them were opened, and they knew that they were naked; and they sewed fig leaves together and made themselves coverings. And they heard the sound of the LORD God walking in the garden in the cool of the day, and Adam and his wife hid themselves from the presence of the LORD God among the trees of the garden. Then the LORD God called to Adam and said to him, 'Where are you?' So he said, 'I heard Your voice in the garden, and I was afraid because I was naked; and I hid myself.' And He said, 'Who told you that you were naked? Have you eaten from the tree of which I commanded you that you should not eat?' Then the man said, 'The woman whom You gave to be with me, she gave me of the tree, and I ate.' And the LORD God said to the woman, 'What is this you have done?' The woman said, 'The serpent deceived me, and I ate.'"

The very sin that caused Satan (Lucifer) to fall is the very sin that Adam and Eve were guilty of: pride (Isaiah 14:12-15). To be prideful is to believe that we know better than God or can live independently of Him. "Every turning from God—for anything—presumes a kind of autonomy or independence that is the essence of pride."[18] When Adam and Eve sinned, they hid from God, as they were ashamed. God was looking for them; it is man who turned away from God. From the very beginning, sin is manifested by our turning away from God and going our own way. Sin separates us from God because by its very nature it is a rejection of God and His will and way.

Two observations can be made regarding the action of Adam and Eve: they doubted the truth of God's word and they chose to believe that God was not good. We cannot have a healthy relationship with anyone if we do not believe what they say or that what they have done or will do is right. Because Satan wants to take the worship from God and be like him (Isaiah 14:13-14), he seeks to destroy our relationship with God by casting doubt on His character so that we do not trust, obey, or depend on Him. In giving the command not to eat of the tree of knowledge of good and evil, God was giving Adam and Eve a boundary: do not go here. To follow this command is to trust Him, believing that He has revealed all that we need to know, that He is not keeping from us anything that we need, and that He does what is good for us and has our best interest at heart.

From the very beginning, God's intention was that we would find in Him what we need. He did not create us to be self-sufficient or independent. Adam and Eve not only doubted God's word, they then acted independently of God. Acting independently from God is the very definition of rebellion against God, and is SIN.

Thank God that He planned a way to resolve the sin problem, through the sacrifice of His Son for all who would believe. "Therefore, just as through one man sin entered into the world, and death by sin, because all sinned... for if by the transgression of the one, the many died, much more did the grace of God and gift by the grace of the one Man, Jesus Christ, abound to the many" (Romans 5:12, 15).

Our relationship with God is only possible through belief in Jesus Christ as Savior and confession of sin. No one, by their own merit alone, can have a relationship with God and have eternal life with Him. Ephesians 2:8-9: "For by grace you have been saved through faith; and that not of yourselves, it is the gift of God; not as a result of works that no one should boast." John 3:16

also tells us: "For God so loved the world, that He gave His only begotten Son, that whosoever believes in Him, should not perish, but have ever lasting life." It is by God's love and grace that we can be saved. In Romans 6:23, we are told that the "wages of sin is death, but the gift of God is eternal life through Jesus Christ our Lord." God's love was demonstrated, "in that while we were still sinners, Christ died for us" (Romans 5:8).

Our salvation is based solely on the person and work of Jesus Christ. If we have acknowledged our sinfulness and inability to save ourselves, and have put our trust in Christ alone for our salvation, then it is not based on anything we have done, it is based on the work and person of Christ. Christ alone makes our salvation sure and makes relationship with Him possible. Once relationship with God has been made possible at salvation, how do we maintain this relationship with Him?

Keys to a Good Relationship with God:

1. Repentance of sin: recognition, owning what we did wrong, confessing it to God, and choosing to not do it again. Repentance at salvation needs to continue throughout the believer's life. "If we confess our sins, He is faithful and just to forgive us our sins and to cleanse us from all unrighteousness. If we say that we have not sinned, we make Him a liar, and His Word is not in us" (1 John 1:9,10) ; "Therefore, having these promises, beloved, let us cleanse ourselves from all filthiness of the flesh and spirit, perfecting holiness in the fear of God... Now I rejoice, not that you were made sorry, but that your sorrow led to repentance. For you were made sorry in a godly manner, that you might suffer loss from us in nothing. For godly sorrow produces repentance leading to salvation, not to be regretted; but the sorrow of the world produces death" (2 Corinthians 7:1, 9-10).

Why Am I So Miserable If This is the Lord's Will

2. Humility (poverty of spirit, Matthew 5:3) which is manifested by: the recognition that no good comes from the flesh (Romans 7:18), and that we cannot please God in or with the flesh (Romans 8:8). Humility is also seen in that we are not only unable to save ourselves; we are unable to sanctify ourselves. "For both He who sanctifies and those who are being sanctified are all of one, for which reason He is not ashamed to call them brethren" (Hebrews 2:11; see John 14:6 and Ephesians 2:8-9 also).

3. Continual dependence on God: once we have recognized our need (humility), also recognizing where our strength comes from: "I will love You, O LORD, my strength" (Psalm 18:1). To not give up, but depend on, God. "Casting all your care upon him; for he cares for you" (1 Peter 5:7). This then requires:

4. Continual obedience, trust (confidence) and faith in God. "Trust in the LORD with all your heart, and lean not on your own understanding; in all your ways acknowledge Him, and He shall direct your paths" (Proverbs 3:5-6). "We ought to obey God rather than men." (Acts 5:29b) "But without faith it is impossible to please Him, for he who comes to God must believe that He is, and that He is a rewarder of those who diligently seek Him" (Hebrews 11:6).

5. Last, but not least: loving God. We cannot rightly obey God without loving God first. "If you love me, keep my commandments" (John 14:15) "...Love the Lord your God with all your heart, with all your soul, and with all your mind. This is the great and foremost commandment" (Matthew 22:37-38). "Whoever keeps His word, truly the love of God is perfected in him" (1 John 2:5).

While a good relationship with God has both been defined by some as loving His Word and others by emotional experience, it will include both.

When we are in fellowship with God, emotional experiences will result; but our relationship with God is defined not by an emotional or intellectual response, but by a response of faith—"without faith it is impossible to please Him" (Hebrews 11:6). Faith always demonstrates dependence on and submission to God, for to have faith is to obey His Word while trusting His promises, character, and enablement.

A relationship with God is only possible when we make the choice to serve Him and not sin. To choose to sin is to cut off fellowship with our Father. Just as the Israelites were exhorted to "choose for yourselves this day whom you will serve" (Joshua 24:15), choosing God is a decision that we either make or do not make every day. The Apostle Paul exhorts us to walk in the Spirit, not according the Flesh (Galatians 5:16).

The flesh will resist submitting to God, and will try to convince us that we will lose our freedom if we do submit to Him. But we cannot lose what we never had to begin with! We are either in bondage to sin, or we are a slave to God. There is no other choice. We serve either one or the other. There is no freedom from service, or from slavery; it is not a question of serving or not serving, but what or whom we will serve.

When the desire of our heart is to serve God, there will be conflict with the desires of the flesh. In our flesh, we walk by sight, not by faith. This is in direct contrast to the description given of a child of God in 2 Corinthians 5:7: "For we walk by faith, not by sight." To trust God when submitting to His will requires believing what He says, while giving up our way, what we want, as well as control, comfort, and convenience. To deny what the flesh wants and do the will of God feels like death, and it is. It is our flesh and its deeds that are dying. This is what is meant passion, evil desire, and covetousness, which is idolatry" (Colossians 3:5) and "For if you live according to the flesh you will die; but if by the Spirit you put to death the deeds of the body, you will live" (Romans 8:13). Note that in Romans is a curious truth: while putting the deeds of the flesh to death feels like death, it is actually life; when we "live it up" in the flesh, we are actually dying.

We are bought with a price; the highest price imaginable. Because of this, we have true freedom; now we can choose who we will serve. We are not bound to sin and death. We can choose life or choose death. We can choose peace or restlessness; joy or listlessness; love or selfishness; the Spirit or the flesh. "I also count all things loss for the excellence of the knowledge of Christ Jesus my Lord, for whom I have suffered the loss of all things, and count them as rubbish, that I may gain Christ" (Philippians 3:8). How can having our own way compare to what we can gain in Christ? We are God's property; He is our master. Will we acknowledge this?

We cannot serve our flesh (ourselves) and serve God at the same time. "No one can serve two masters; for either he will hate the one and love the other, or else he will be loyal to the one and despise the other." (Matthew 6:24) God did not save us to enable us to become more self-sufficient or to legitimize living in our own strength, according to our own will. He saved us to free us from the bondage to self and sin, not to support it! He saved us by revealing to us our need for salvation and our total inability to save ourselves; why do we think that we have the ability to sanctify ourselves? "This only I want to learn from you: Did you receive the Spirit by the works of the law or by the hearing of faith? Are you so foolish? Having begun in the Spirit, are you now being made perfect by the flesh?" (Galatians 3:2-3) "He who began a good work in you will complete it" (Philippians 1:6).

When we attempt to do God's work in our own strength, in our own way or own time, it does not matter what we are trying to do, it is not God's work. This is why we cannot define our relationship with God by **what** we are doing. If what we are doing is being done in our way and by our means, how is God being honored and glorified? There cannot be a good relationship with God if what we are doing is not being done for His glory and by His Spirit. No matter how "good" a work is, if it is being done in our strength, according to our way and means, it is a work that will only be consumed at the judgment seat of Christ:

> *"So then neither he who plants is anything, nor he who waters, but God who gives the increase...I have laid the foundation, and another builds on it. But let each one take heed how he builds on it. For no other foundation can anyone lay than that which is laid, which is Jesus Christ. Now if anyone builds on this foundation with gold, silver, precious stones, wood, hay, straw, each one's work will become clear; for the Day will declare it, because it will be revealed by fire; and the fire will test each one's work, of what sort it is. If anyone's work which he has built endures, he will receive a reward. If anyone's work is burned, he will suffer loss; but he himself will be saved, yet so as through fire" (1 Corinthians 3:7, 10-15).*

Not only do we lose out on heavenly rewards when we walk according to the flesh, we also lose what blessings are available to us now that can only come from a right relationship with God (Galatians 5:22-23). To operate independently from God is to turn away from peace, joy, love, comfort, strength and healing. The only time God is honored and truly obeyed is when we depend on Him, wait on Him, and follow His Word. It is all about what He wants, and how He wants it done; our agendas, prerogatives and will have been submitted to His. It matters to God not only **what** we are doing, but **why** and **how** we are doing it.

The more we keep trying to make things work out through fleshly efforts, the more life is and will become a struggle. This struggle is resolved by surrendering our will, way and means to God and accept what He has provided, the means He has determined (as detailed in His Word), and the circumstances He has allowed in our lives. It also means putting aside whatever expectations we have of what serving Him means or what determines success.

In other words, total surrender of our will and way to the Lord. The way God measures success and determines service is quite different than what our flesh wants or would do. The flesh defines success as being recognized and praised by others. Faithful service especially is seen as that which produces results. Yet this is not God's viewpoint at all. Success in God's eyes is not necessarily measured by results; it is determined by our attitude toward God, and whether we are living in obedience to Him and His Word. God does not measure faithful service as that which only comes about from "full-time" Christian service (from only missionaries and pastors). It does not have to be something visible and measurable from human perspective. Serving God faithfully is simply that: doing His will, living in submission to His Word. It is demonstrated through obedience, trust, prayer, and ministry to others.

Because of what Christ has done for us, we are able to choose to know and obey God. Our relationship with God is strengthened and maintained when we choose each day to praise and exalt Him above all else; to humble ourselves before Him, and love Him with our whole heart, soul, and mind. But, if anything other than God is first in our lives, then that is what we are serving. When we serve anything other than God, our relationship with God is going to be disabled. When we sin, the good news is God has provided a way for our relationship with Him to be restored. The solution is simple, but not easy: repentance (1 John 1:9). Though this has been mentioned before, it bears repeating. Repentance is not just for unbelievers; repentance is continually needed for the believer, as we sin every day. We may have blind spots regarding the things we do; we may be more aware of being in a bad mood, or being upset and angry about something. When we are discontent or bitter, usually there is sin as the cause, and we are out of fellowship with God. Though we always have the Holy Spirit who convicts us of our sin, we can become desensitized to our sinful behavior. If we don't know what the problem is, ask Him to reveal it. Once we repent, we will see how quickly feelings change.

We must see the inadequacy of our ways and the depravity of our sin and all sin; to repent is to see our sin the way God sees it, and to turn from it to Him. Repentance is to confess our sin, be forgiven, and to stop doing what is wrong to start doing what is right. Repentance of sin, humility, thankfulness and praise are what enable us to abide in Christ and walk in the Spirit. (John 15:4-11; 1 Peter 5:6-7; Philippians 4:4-6).

When we walk in the Spirit (Galatians 5:16) we will display the fruit of the Spirit (Galatians 5:22-23). We do not have to develop the fruit of the Spirit in our lives. God produces the fruit of the Spirit in our lives when we walk in the Spirit, but walking in the Spirit is not possible if there is sin in our lives. It cannot be all about us and what we want, and be about God and what He wants at the same time. "If anyone desires to come after me, let him deny himself, take up his cross, and follow me" (Matthew 16:24). Ask: Am I doing what is right in order to get something in return from God? (If I do this, God is obligated to do that). Are we serving self, or God?

Walking in the Spirit does not happen automatically. It is not modus operandi. The tendency to serve self or the flesh is a daily battle that can only be won with complete dependence on God. This is a process which takes time. Even when we pray and read His Word on a regular basis, we may find ourselves either falling into old habits or developing some new bad ones! Do not be disheartened or discouraged. The flesh never changes and will resist being denied. The closer we walk with God, the more intense temptation and trial can become (demanding ever greater dependence on God).

An indication of spiritual growth and maturity is how quickly we realize we are not walking in the Spirit, but in the flesh, and how quickly we seek to remedy the situation. The longer we ignore the prompting of the Spirit, the more disabled our relationship with Him will become. Walking in the Spirit requires discipline, for we must choose between what the flesh wants and what the Spirit wants. This often requires ignoring how we feel, and trusting God to take care of us even if we don't like what He is allowing.

Why Am I So Miserable If This is the Lord's Will

Instead of bringing "every thought into captivity" (2 Corinthians 10:5) we want to spend time with God when it is convenient for us, i.e., when we can make time for it, or when we feel like doing it. Instead of scheduling our life around God, God gets scheduled into our lives, when and where we can fit Him in. If there isn't enough time, something needs to be cut. Even mothers with small children can include God in their day, talking to Him and praising Him while they are doing something else. We need to evaluate our priorities. Is there anything we are doing where God can't be included in the activity? Is there anything that prevents us from having time with Him?

People who are pressed for time protest that they cannot make the time for God when they need it most of all. Giving God our time when we don't have any is like giving God a tithe when there isn't any money left over. It requires faith. It is trusting God to make it all work out if we give sacrificially to Him. He always works it out; perhaps not in the way we think or hope He will; most times, He does more than I expect. We cannot out-give God. Those who are willing to step out in faith, trusting His provision, will always be blessed spiritually.

Do we share our heart with the Lord? Do we tell Him what is on our mind and what we are struggling with or what we are thankful for? Do we praise Him and thank Him when we are not in a church service? When we pray, is it just a list? Lists are not necessarily wrong; they can help us remember everything and everyone who needs prayer. But think about it: when we go out with a friend for a lunch date, do we bring a list or do we just share our heart with one another? God wants us to talk to Him. Each day we need to recognize that apart from Him, we can do nothing (John 15:5). There isn't anything that is too small or too big for God to do—and he is never bothered when we go to Him. Honesty is not going to shock Him—can we say anything that He does not already know about? If angry, respectfully tell Him. Ask Him for ever-increasing love for Him and to be controlled by His Spirit and not by your feelings.

If we are not sharing our heart and life with God on a regular basis (talking and listening to Him), our relationship with Him will suffer and stagnate. We may be going through all the motions: attending church and even serving in church, but there will be no joy, contentment, satisfaction, or true peace. Many do not notice the lack of these because it has been so long since they experienced them.

Do we listen to God? This means taking time in our devotions to sit and be quiet before Him. I have never heard an audible voice from God and don't expect to until I get to heaven. But there have been many times when I have been struggling with an issue that after I have waited on Him He has ministered to me in some way by bringing a Scripture passage or hymn to mind, or comfort through the Holy Spirit. When we read and meditate on the Word of God, are we listening to it? To listen is "to hear something with thoughtful attention: give consideration."[19]

We place value on the Word of God when we listen to and apply it. If we wait until we feel like reading the Word, it will rarely happen. The flesh will never encourage us to sit down and read it. Reading God's Word is much more than just an intellectual exercise; it is God communicating to us what we need to know to have a relationship with Him and have an abundant spiritual life. "All Scripture is given by inspiration of God, and is profitable for doctrine, for reproof, for correction, for instruction in righteousness" (2 Timothy 3:16).

Praying and Bible study should not become a formula followed for spiritual success, a routine to make us a good Christian. Giving time to the Lord in the morning provides the opportunity to make Him the focus of our day. Praying and Bible study does not make this automatic, but it does give us the means by which it can happen. The supernatural only happens supernaturally! Making God the priority in our lives is a choice. We will either go through the motions or choose to exalt the Lord and make Him what we live for.

Why Am I So Miserable If This is the Lord's Will

So what are the consequences of not being in consistent fellowship with God? We may not see the need for change; things seem to be fine the way they are. And we may not see a need to change, really. We attend church, hear a sermon, and sing a song. We have friends at church, and think we have good fellowship. This is what the Christian life is all about isn't it? If this is all that our spiritual life is about, we are only skimming the surface. Worse yet, we are depriving ourselves from experiencing God and His blessings. The more we neglect our relationship with God, the more we depend on the flesh. Neglecting our relationship with God is not simply missing out on blessings, on knowing God; it is to our peril if we do so. When we rely on anything other than God for strength, wisdom, insight, comfort, peace, protection or help, we are going to be let down, disappointed, deceived, led astray, hurt or damaged.

Anytime we start feeling restless, irritable, or miserable, it is an indication that we have started to depend on our flesh to meet our needs instead of God. We need to recognize who or what is causing us distress. It isn't location, culture, people, church, job, employer, marriage, singleness, or any other circumstance. These are only symptoms of the real problem — a disconnection with God. When satisfaction is found in the Lord, anything this world offers is irrelevant. The things we enjoy can only be enjoyed when they are complimentary to what the Lord provides and honors Him; when it is painful, He provides all the resources we need.

Knowing this, why don't we go to God? Why do we get disconnected?

1. We think we are already with Him
2. Our emotional and physical desires are for something or someone other than God
3. We don't believe that all of our needs can be met in God

4. We think doing things God's way means going without enjoyment in life

Only in Him do we have true peace and contentment; believing the lie that someone or something else can meet a need that God cannot fill destroys our fellowship with Him. If our needs are not being met in Him, we will look for them to be met in others. Are our expectations of people, church, job, etc. unrealistic? Are they unreasonable? Why do we expect so much? Can other people read our mind? Is there a set of circumstances in which we will find continual happiness? Are we always looking for something better, instead of thanking God for what we have?

Everyone is needy. God created us with a desire for relationship. When we go to others for the acceptance, understanding, affirmation, and encouragement that only God can provide, we place too much responsibility on them; they will only be overwhelmed and we will be disappointed. People have limitations that prevent them from being and doing what we hope they will be and do. A person or people may seem to be just what we need, but they cannot always be there when we need them. It is not physically or practically possible. Only God promises to never leave us: "I will never leave you or forsake you" (Hebrews 13:5).

When we are in a right relationship with Him, we are then in the best position possible to have relationships with others. Our relationships with others will reflect our relationship with Him: if we submit to God, we will submit to others; if we love God, we will love others. When our needs are met in Him, we no longer demand that others meet them; relationships become about sharing with them, experiencing things with them. But if we are disconnected from God, our relationships with others suffer, because we end up putting demands on them that only God can fill.

Constantly seeking something better down here is chasing after the wind. "I have seen all the works that are done under the sun; and indeed, all is vanity and grasping for the wind." (Ecclesiastes 1:14). It does not matter what it is: friends, husband/wife, pleasure, job and so forth. Those who constantly seek after something better through earthly means are convinced that they have needs that aren't being met. "My God shall supply all your need according to His riches …" (Philippians 4:19) is often misinterpreted or misunderstood. There are two key terms in this verse at issue: need and supply. The literal interpretation of need is that which is only necessary. The item desired is necessary for sustenance (Thayer's Lexicon). What we may think is a need may be something we can live without; it may also simply be a want, a desire of the flesh. God may allow circumstances in our lives in which we are deprived of what we consider necessary, so as to test our faith and trust in Him.

The definition for supply is to fill or fill up, but the problem with supply is not the definition, but **what we expect to be supplied with.** We know that we are supplied "according to His riches." That tells us how as well as the extent of the source of the supply (infinite). It does not tell us in what way God will supply the need, or in what time He will supply the need. If it is a true need, and not just a fleshly desire, God will meet it if we trust and wait on Him. While we wait on Him, depending on Him, we are responsible for being good stewards of the time, talents, and possessions God has given us: "As each one has received a gift, minister it to one another, as good stewards of the manifold grace of God" (1 Peter 4:10). The parable of the steward in Luke 16 and the parable of the talents in Matthew 25:14-29 also support this.

When we are in circumstances beyond our control, and have done all we can do, then it is up to God to provide. This is when we are tested in our faith: will we still believe that He is good, that He loves us if there is a delay and we don't get what we want or need when we want it? Anything that we want or have, whether it is a possession, person, or place, that we are convinced we cannot live without, has become our god. If God is not giving us what we want, it is not a punishment! It is His grace. He is our Creator. He alone can satisfy our soul. He alone can claim to supply our need, for He alone knows what we need. He always loves, is true and faithful. Being in the Lord's will does not mean that He is or will provide for us the way we expect or hope He will, but He always takes care of us in a way that will sustain us with joy. This is what the journey of our Christian life is all about: learning to trust that His way is best, even if we cannot see how our needs are going to be met.

The flesh will never crave time with God. We need to recognize that when we do not want or feel like spending time with God or doing that which glorifies Him, this is of the flesh. Ignore it. Turn away from it; choose to depend on God for help and strength to do His will. It does not matter what our flesh feels like doing, or what we think "has to" get done; giving our feelings priority will not give us the emotional resolution that we crave. Ironically, it is only when we stop any attempt on our part to achieve comfort, control and convenience through our plans, schemes, agendas, methods and manipulations, and instead trust God to take care of us, that we find what we were looking for but never achieved in our own way and strength.

The question now is what choice will we make. Once we start thinking about the choices we make, the motivations behind them start to become apparent. Do we live for TV, sports, books, fun, and food for pleasure? Or do we live for God and being in fellowship with Him? What do we consider essential for enjoying life, making life worthwhile? Anything other than God may make us feel good at the moment, but is never sufficient; it only makes us miserable in the end.

Living by the Spirit does not mean giving up all enjoyment of life. On the contrary, life is best enjoyed when it is lived the way God intended it, within the parameters He has given us. It does not mean total abstinence of anything and everything remotely enjoyable, like living like a monk from the 13th century. When it is not always clear what to do, we can pray and ask for

Why Am I So Miserable If This is the Lord's Will

discernment; we can also ask someone who is spiritually mature. The reason why we need discernment in determining what we do for fun, how we work and so forth, is because we have a tendency to convince ourselves that what we want to do is alright. That is why we need to look into the mirror that is God's Word and humble ourselves in prayer.

When a person's priorities are skewed, their whole approach to Christian living is wrong. When priorities are out of order, emotional or physical well-being is emphasized at the expense of the spiritual. When emotions or physical desires are being served, Christians find they are doing things for the wrong reasons or following the wrong people or teachings. While living according to the Spirit may seem at times like a lack of provision for the emotional and physical, quite the opposite is true. God truly knows what we need, much better than we do. The Creator knows what His creation needs; submitting to Him always reveals that.

It is sad to realize that there are those who have been serving the wrong thing or person for years. When they begin to realize that they have been doing things in the wrong way, or for the wrong reason, it can be very tempting for them to ignore or deny the error. Facing their error and changing their ways may mean upheaval in their lives; what will everyone think? Can this really be all that bad? It may not be an outright denial: "I didn't do anything wrong!" Rather, it may simply be a denial of the consequences of their error. But to ignore or deny sin is to continue in it. As long as we refuse to submit to God and obey Him, and repent of our sin, we will never know God's forgiveness and peace.

The quality of our relationship with God is indicated in the degree to which we depend upon Him and trust Him, how we respond to His Word, and the circumstances in our life. Our relationship with Him is directly proportional to the faith we have in Him, and the love we have for Him; it will be evidenced by the fruit of the Spirit. We can do many "good" things and yet be doing them for the wrong reasons. To serve God with the right reason is to serve Him out of love: "Love the Lord your God with all your heart..." (Matthew 22:37).

Loving God

"Holy, holy, holy is the LORD of hosts; the whole earth is full of His glory!" (Isaiah 6:3)

"Oh, sing to the LORD a new song! For He has done marvelous things; His right hand and His holy arm have gained Him the victory" (Psalm 98:1).

"Therefore, you shall love the Lord your God" (Deuteronomy 11:1a). What does it mean to love God? How we define this, and how we are to love Him, is based solely on the complete revelation of truth about Himself in His Word. To define God by our idea of what we want God to be, or by what we understand love to be, will lead to worship of a god of our own making. It is true that God is love and is gracious, but if we ignore other attributes that make us uncomfortable, we will not have a clear, concise, or complete picture of who He is. To love God is to accept and embrace all that is revealed about Him in His Word, worshipping and praising Him for all of His attributes.

What does God's Word tell us about loving Him? How do we know when we love Him? "If you love me, keep my commandments" (John 14:15). Loving God will result in obedience to His Word. "But whoever keeps His word, truly the love of God is perfected in him. By this we know that we are in Him" (1 John 2:5). This does not mean that loving God is just an action, something that we do. Loving God encompasses every aspect of our being; obedience to His Word results from a love that involves our whole heart, soul,

Why Am I So Miserable If This is the Lord's Will

mind, and strength (Mark 12:30). Our love for God is not only an emotional response, it is a determination of mind and will that we obey, serve, love and trust Him, no matter how we feel or what circumstances befall us. We are able to make this choice only by depending on Him.

Loving God is the whole of Christian living. It is not part of Christian living, or simply one of the things on our list of "must dos" (read the Bible, pray, etc.); it is **all**. Everything we do—evangelism, holiness, growth, serving others—is to be rooted in and motivated by our love for God. If it is not, it is rooted in something else, which not only makes it meaningless, but dishonors God. When love for God is the force and motivation behind what we do, it will be demonstrated by obedience and submission to Him and His Word in all things, not just the things we have decided to obey.

We are to love God not because of the gifts or blessings that He gives, but because of who He is. If not for who He is, there would be no creation, no salvation, no Savior, no sanctification, no glorification, no kingdom, no New Jerusalem, no true blessing of any kind. To focus on the blessings we want, and do what we think is required to get them, is not to love God but the gifts He gives. We may think we love God, but if our focus is on what He gives, rather than on who He is, we worship and love something other than God. Even if outwardly we are giving lip service to Him, if what we are doing is to earn blessings, it is a work being done for what **we** get out of it. That is self-love and self-worship. How can there be a love for God unless He is the focus?

Loving God is to put 1 Corinthians 13 in action toward Him. To love God is to exalt God and not self; it is to always believe and hope in Him despite whatever trials or difficult circumstances we have to endure. When we love Him, we place no value on our own safety or comfort, but on His glory and honor in all things, believing that God will take care of us (Psalm 55:22; Hebrews 13:5). We cannot say that we love God if we place a higher priority on avoiding that which is painful, uncomfortable or inconvenient, than on obeying, trusting serving, and depending on Him in any circumstance. Loving God is to believe that He allows what is in our best interest, even if we do not see how it can be. We do not fear trial or tribulation, because we know that whatever God allows to come our way, He will enable us to get through it; not only that, we know that He will bring good out of it (1 Corinthians 10:13; Romans 8:28).

The foundation of a love for God is a thankful, grateful, humble heart full of praise. God's Word is filled with praise in the Psalms written by David and others that love Him; commands are given for humility ("Therefore humble yourselves under the mighty hand of God," 1 Peter 5:6), and thankfulness ("Be anxious for nothing, but in everything by prayer and supplication, with thanksgiving, let your requests be known unto God" Philippians 4:6). When our love for God is supported by humility and thankfulness, it will be demonstrated by believing in Him in spite of our circumstances, and praising Him for His provision before we can see it. Love, then, results in faith: "Now faith is the substance of things hoped for, the evidence of things not seen" (Hebrews 11:1). How is this love possible? It is possible because anyone born of God loves God. 1 John 4:7-8 tell us: "Beloved, let us love one another, for love is of God; and everyone who loves is born of God and knows God. He who does not love does not know God, for God is love." In verse 19 of the same chapter John also tells us: "We love Him because He first loved us." Loving God is possible because God himself made it possible when He made us one of His children.

Our priority is to love God; second, is to love others (Matthew 27:37-39; Mark 12:30, Luke 10:37). Sincere love for others can only take place when God has first place in our hearts and lives. He is our source; He is everything we need. He makes truly loving others possible. "A new commandment I give to you, that you love one another, even as I have loved you that you also love one another. By this, all men will know that you are my disciples, if you have love for one another" (John 13:34-35). When we are loved by God, we are then enabled to love others without needing or expecting anything in return. "If we love one another, God abides in us, and His love has been perfected in us" (1 John 4:12). Philippians 2:3 reminds us to "Let nothing be done through selfish ambition or conceit, but in lowliness of mind let each esteem others better than himself."

Whomever or whatever we give the priority to in our life is our god. To make other people or another person our god is the most unloving thing we can do to them. To "love" someone more than we love God means we depend on and serve them more than we do God. No one wants that kind of expectation. If we love others biblically, we do not want to burden anyone; we want to assist them in any way that we can, particularly in their relationship with God. Love, as expressed in 1 Corinthians 13, is not about how someone else makes us feel, or about being co-dependent with someone else; it isn't about what the other person does for us at all.

To make love for people our priority, and not love for God, is to be focused on gaining approval from people, not God; to love God's Word, and not people is to love truth and being right rather than loving people or God. In either case, we have let our natural inclination (social or intellectual) determine how we will serve God. But when we love God, we will love what He loves and will obey Him and serve Him according to His terms. We will not pick or choose what statutes we will obey. Am I going to demand that I serve God only on my terms? To do so is not to serve Him at all.

Not only can other people become the focus of our service, our love for God can get misplaced. A passion for finding and correcting error can become an obsession; we end up exalting the means to the relationship with God (His Word) rather than God Himself. We want to make sure that God's Word is accurately represented; but when it becomes what we serve, rather than God, it leads to legalism. 1 Corinthians 13:2 states: "And though I have the gift of prophecy, and understand all mysteries and all knowledge, and though I have all faith, so that I could remove mountains, but have not love, I am nothing."

When we love God, we will care about what He cares about (His Word, His people, His will) and will hate what He hates (lies, deception, pride). As we walk in obedience to His Word out of our love for Him, the more we will grow in our love for Him and for what He loves, and the more we will hate what He hates. How very precious is God's Word; God has given it to us, to reveal Himself, and to give us all we need to know to live in right relationship with Him. How we respond to His Word will indicate our love for Him. Do we repent our sins? Trust Him? Obey Him? Follow Him? Depend on Him? Love His Word? Love people? If not, we love ourselves or something or someone else.

God's Word

For the Word of God is living and powerful, and sharper than any two-edged sword, piercing even to the division of soul and spirit, and of joints and marrow, and is a discerner of the thoughts and intents of the heart. (Hebrews 4:12)

For the LORD is good; His mercy is everlasting, and His truth endures to all generations. (Psalm 100:5)

The entirety of Your word is truth, and every one of Your righteous judgments endures forever. (Psalm 119:160)

God is the source of truth. Jesus said, "I am the way, the *truth*, and the life." (John 14:6a) If He is truth, then truth (whatever knowledge He has given in His Word) is going to be consistent with who He is: constant, eternal, perfect, infallible, complete, and absolute. It is also going to be exclusive; only God is truth, and what He says is truth. Defining truth to be relative or subjective is to reject God as the source of truth. As a result, we will be unwilling to submit to His Word in all areas of our life; sin is downplayed or redefined altogether. Since we do not want anyone to hold us accountable to the standards of God's Word, holding other people accountable will be defined as being "judgmental" and worse than any other sin. Yet Galatians 6:1 says: "Brethren, if a man is overtaken in any trespass, you who are spiritual, restore such a one in a spirit of gentleness." Matthew 18:15-18 details how an erring brother is restored; note that it includes holding them responsible for their action, confronting them, and what to do if they do not repent.

To reject the truth that God has given us in His Word is to reject Him. We must not allow the popular definition of truth that the world is propagating to lead us astray. To say we believe in God, and not believe what God has revealed about Himself in His Word, and what He teaches us about sin, salvation, and spiritual life, is to believe in some other god than the God of the Bible; a god of our own making.

Accepting the world's definition of truth makes God's truth shameful. "For whoever is ashamed of me and my words, of him will the Son of Man be ashamed when He comes in His glory, and the glory of the Father and of the holy angels" (Luke 9:26). It is always good to speak it, meditate on it, and memorize it. Love is always the rule (1 Corinthians 13). We do not love when we will not speak the truth for fear of hurting others. Love wants what is best for others, even if it includes pain. Love recognizes that pain is not the worst thing that can happen to a person, being separated from God is.

God is truth. We know what truth is when we walk according to the Spirit and abide in Him. To walk according to the flesh means that I determine what is truth. I put myself in God's place. Why do we do this? Because acknowledging God's truth means denying the flesh and what it demands. It means having to: 1) give up our way, will, or agenda to the Lord; 2) Give up what feels good at the moment; and 3) trust God when we can't see what He says is true. We choose to define what truth is so that we can avoid that which is painful or uncomfortable. But to make this choice is to deceive ourselves, for there is no truth except God's truth. The flesh's attempt in avoiding pain and discomfort will always ultimately fail; we not only do not get what we were aiming for, but we also lose out on all the blessings that come from submission to God.

We may think that we have received special insight from God on a matter. It may be that we have, by God's grace, come to understand a truth from God that we had not understood before. When this happens, it can be such a revelation that we think "This is it! I get the whole picture now!" But this is not possible, because "For now we see in a mirror, dimly, but then face to face. Now I know in part, but then I shall know just as I also am known" (1 Corinthians 13:12).

We need to compare what we are learning with Scripture. As much as we are sure that what we have received is of God, we need to check to see that it is consistent with God's Word. Being firmly rooted in God's truth and applying it correctly and lovingly is obtained when: 1) we properly use and interpret it, seeking to understand portions of Scripture in relation to the context; 2) we depend on God to lead us, guide us in when and what we should say, and not letting fear of rejection or hurt keep us from doing His will; and 3) when truth is not our obsession, God is. We love His truth because we love Him; we do not love Him because we love His truth. When truth is what we worship, serve, and love, we will not have the love we ought to have for God, and definitely not what we need to have for others.

Part of God's Word is His law. David says: "O how I love thy law! It is my meditation all the day" (Psalm 119:97). As a child, I wondered how anyone can love a list of rules. How could David love the law of God? He gives the reason in v.98-100, 104, 113-114, and 165 of the same chapter:

"Your commandments make me wiser than my enemies, for they are ever with me. I have more understanding than all my teachers, for your testimonies are my meditation. I understand more than the ancients, because I keep Your precepts... from Your precepts I get understanding; therefore I hate every false way... I hate the double-minded, but I love Your law. You are my hiding place and my shield; I wait for Your Word... great peace have those who love Your law, and nothing causes them to stumble."

David did not look at obeying God's law as not being able to do what he wanted to do. By the testimony just given, David saw it as God's formula for understanding, insight, and peace. He viewed it as enabling, not preventing, his enjoyment of life. Psalm 19:7-11 tells us:

"The law of the Lord is perfect, converting the soul; the testimony of the Lord is sure, making wise the simple. The precepts of the Lord are right, rejoicing the heart: the commandment of the Lord is pure, enlightening the eyes. The fear of the Lord is clean, enduring forever; the judgments of the Lord are true; they are righteous altogether. More to be desired are they than gold, yea, than much fine gold; sweeter also than honey and the honeycomb. Moreover by them Your servant is warned; and in keeping them there is great reward."

Why did David delight in God's law? Because it was God's instructions to Him to keep him from harm and to give him what was good. David understood that what harmed him most of all was sin; God's law revealed that sin to him, giving him opportunity to repent. How did He come to this understanding? By meditating on the law of God, David thought about the purpose of the law, and what it accomplishes; in so doing, he was meditating

The Flesh & Our Relationship with God   123 on God, on what God has done, who He is, and what He wants for us. He loved God's law, for it was an expression of God's love to us; it showed God's intent for our protection, insight, and good.

God's law is not restricting us from anything that is good for us; rather, it keeps us from harm. On the contrary, the law's ultimate purpose is to reveal our need of God! May we like David cry: "Open my eyes that I may behold wonderful things from Thy law!" (Psalm 119:18) God's law, His holy Word is an invaluable resource. It gives us the standard for evaluating right from wrong; it reveals the character of God and what He has done for us; it strengthens, encourages, supports, helps, corrects, and chastens us. Most importantly, it provides the means by which a relationship with God is begun and is the guide for maintaining that relationship. Romans 10:17 tells of the start of the relationship: "Faith comes from hearing and hearing by the word of Christ." One of the verses I learned as a child speaks to how His Word guides: "Thy Word is a lamp to my feet and a light to my path" (Psalm 119:105).

This being said, while most Christians would agree as to the importance of the Word of God, it may not be the basis of their "spiritual" experience; it is not trusted, believed or relied upon.

Experience vs. Scripture

"But I fear, lest somehow, as the serpent deceived Eve by his craftiness, so your minds may be corrupted from the simplicity that is in Christ. For if he who comes preaches another Jesus whom we have not preached, or if you receive a different spirit which you have not received, or a different gospel which you have not accepted—you may well put up with it!" (2 Corinthians 11:3-5)

So what is so wrong about trusting an experience of God? It is wrong when that experience is what determines truth for us. God has communicated to us what is true **in His Word.** What does it mean that God's Word is true? The Bible speaks for itself: "All Scripture is given by inspiration of God, and is profitable for doctrine, for reproof, for correction, for instruction in righteousness" (2 Timothy 3:16). We believe that every word is inspired. If all Scripture is God-breathed, then it becomes the standard for truth: "Every word of God is pure" (Proverbs 30:5).

The problem with relying on experience is that we may give it equal authority with the Word of God. Experience, rather than the Word of God itself, is often used as the means for interpreting and understanding the Scriptures, or it is used as the standard of truth apart from the Scriptures. Some believers are so sure that what they have experienced is from God, that the experience is preferred over or used in addition to the Word of God.

As mentioned earlier, God's Word testifies of itself that it is true; God does not contradict Himself. He will not tell anyone to steal, lie, or gossip, or reveal any truth through an experience that would contradict His Word. Yet there are believers who value only what they experience; even when that experience cannot be supported by Scripture. To trust experience in place of God's Word will result in false doctrine. False doctrine is not just that which blatantly rejects Christ; most false doctrine simply mixes what is false with truth. The result: an improper view and understanding of who God is and how He operates. For them, what is right is based on their understanding and experience, not what God has revealed in His Word.

When experience is used as a standard for truth we will come to wrong conclusions, and wrong interpretations of events around us. God is the source of truth; only He can give the right perspective on life. When we base our expectations on our experience, and not on God's Word or character, our perception will not be based on truth, but on a lie. In so doing, we only set ourselves up for being hurt, bitter, and angry with God. We will think God is at fault, when it is our expectations that are all wrong. God says: "For My thoughts are not your thoughts, nor are your ways My ways" (Isaiah 55:8). We cannot expect to fully grasp all that He is or to understand how and why He does all that He does. Walking by faith is all about trusting that God is good, that He can be trusted, even when we cannot see how at the moment.

How we live demonstrates what we really believe. Biblical doctrine is to believe what God says in His Word about God, Jesus, the Holy Spirit, Creation, salvation, the Church, etc. Doctrine matters to all Christians, for correct doctrine is the basis for correct practice. God's Word exhorts us not to neglect doctrine: "Meditate on these things; give yourself entirely to them, that your progress may be evident to all. Take heed to yourself and to the doctrine. Continue in them, for in doing this you will save both yourself and those who hear you" (1 Timothy 4:15-16).

When interpreting God's Word, it is important to remember that literal interpretation includes metaphors, similes and so forth. Those who spiritualize a text either give a Bible passage more meaning than a literal rendering of the passage gives, or reject the literal meaning and replace it with another interpretation. Spiritualizing a text can be very dangerous. This is because once we go beyond what the passage says (word for word) to what we think it means, the basis for truth is no longer on God but on our understanding. But, if our understanding is based on other Scriptures and we are using other Scripture to understand the passage, then the basis for truth and understanding is Scripture, not us. We need to be very careful that any conclusion that we come to is a result of truth from the Word of God, not on something that simply seems right.

Bible study is important for every Christian because: 1) we are easily led astray by false doctrine ("...tossed to and fro and carried about with every wind of doctrine, by the trickery of men, in the cunning craftiness of deceitful plotting" [Ephesians 4:14]); and 2) without it we will not have the proper foundation for the choices that need to be made every day. Knowing and understanding what we believe about God, what He has done for us, and what He will do is of vital importance, for what we believe directly impacts our relationship with God and others, as well as how we live.

Experience of God is essential to our spiritual growth. To simply learn something intellectually only gives us factual knowledge; it will not and cannot give us experiential knowledge of God. But an experience can be a result of human insight, desire, or emotion, or it can be a result of an encounter with God; that is why the Word of God is vital to evaluating whether the experience is of God or of the flesh. It is the Word of God that the Spirit of God uses to give us discernment, enabling us to evaluate what is right and wrong, what is good, and what is evil. Any true experience of God will be in harmony with the truth in His Word. To experience or understand something about God not found in His Word is not of God.

Spiritual Discernment

And this I pray, that your love may abound still more and more in knowledge and all discernment. (Philippians 1:9)

We cannot enable anyone to understand a spiritual truth, for truth in God's Word can only be spiritually discerned. "But the natural man does not receive the things of the Spirit of God, for they are foolishness to him; nor can he know them, because they are spiritually discerned" (1 Corinthians 2:14). Ephesians 1:17-19 also describes: "That the God of our Lord Jesus Christ, the Father of glory, may give to you the spirit of wisdom and revelation in the knowledge of

Him, the eyes of your understanding being enlightened; that you may know what is the hope of His calling." Only God reveals truth. Acts 26:17-18 describes the necessity of God opening eyes (giving spiritual sight and understanding) so that the Gentiles would believe. Other passages refer to the Lord enlightening their eyes or heart, or to a plea to God for Him to enlighten them (2 Samuel 22:29; Ezra 9:8; Job 33:30; Psalm 13:3, 18:28).

We need to be careful that we do not mistake intellectual comprehension with spiritual understanding; just because we think we understand, it does not mean that we do. Young believers, having been taught a lot of Bible knowledge, may no longer have a teachable spirit, thinking that there is nothing new to learn. But God's Word is so much more than a textbook or history lesson. It is "living and powerful, sharper than any two-edged sword" (Hebrews 4:12). One of the ways we receive spiritual understanding or discernment is when He reveals to us the meaning and application of a truth from His Word through a trial or temptation. This is the "ah-ha!" moment, where His Word becomes alive. We find ourselves saying "so that's what that meant... ." We thought we knew it before, but then realize we really didn't. Spiritual discernment is only made possible with God. "If any of you lacks wisdom, let him ask of God" (James 1:5a).

If a believer lacks spiritual discernment there are three possible causes: 1) willful sin; 2) level of spiritual maturity or growth; or 3) lack of dependence on God. Willful sin will block fellowship with God. "If I regard iniquity in my heart, the Lord will not hear" (Psalm 66:18). A new believer will not have as much discernment as a more mature believer will have, for discernment comes as the believer walks by faith during various trials and temptations. Lack of dependence on God is not always a conscious choice of the will; more often than not, it is due to just doing what comes naturally, which is sin. Whether it is known or unknown sin, asking God for wisdom will address this and reveal the need for repentance. If there is no sin, asking him for insight demonstrates our dependence on Him and brings Him glory.

When God has revealed the truth of His Word to us, and we experience Him, we will have an intense desire for others to experience the same thing. When we share what we have learned, we need to depend on the Spirit of God to reveal it to them. While we cannot reveal spiritual truth to others, we can demonstrate the love of God to them, and we can pray that God will open their eyes. A hunger and love for God only develops as each person responds to the Spirit of God.

"But I tell you who hear me: Love your enemies, do good to those who hate you, bless those who curse you, pray for those who mistreat you. If someone strikes you on one cheek, turn to him the other also. If someone takes your cloak, do not stop him from taking your tunic. Give to everyone who asks you, and if anyone takes what belongs to you, do not demand it back. Do to others as you would have them do to you."

– Luke 6.27-31

"Are you willing to choose to relinquish your life, to die to yourself, so that God's love can be released through you to those He has called you to love? Are you willing to choose to love others before or instead of yourself?"[20]

Chapter 6
The Flesh & Our Relationship with Others

*B*eing dependent on God, having all sufficiency from Him, does not mean that we do not need other people. It does mean that we do not have to have their approval or acceptance, or rely on them to meet our emotional needs. When we no longer have to make demands of others, or feel the need to please, we are able to love and communicate with others freely, without expectation or need for reciprocation. When our needs are met in Christ, we are free to love others and support them in their walk in the Spirit.

God uses other people in our lives to draw us closer to Him. Those who irritate can teach us to rely on Him more for the love, grace, forgiveness, and patience we need. Those who are in fellowship with God can bless us with encouragement, exhortation, and instruction. God teaches us through godly and ungodly people.

When we have our needs met in God, we no longer need to "suck the life" out of other people. When our needs are **not** met in Him, we will look elsewhere, and become takers instead of givers. This does not enable good relationships, but disables them. The basis for healthy relationships is a healthy relationship with God. When the basis for our relationship with others is what they do for us, or having our needs met, our focus is on us. We can never get the amount or quality of attention that we crave from others, for everyone is limited and fallible; only God is and can be there at all times, in perfect love. This is the crux of the matter—relationships with others that satisfy must be pursued God's way, depending on Him for the enabling. God's way is about love, for God is love (1 John 4:8). Since love does not seek its own (1 Corinthians 13:5), relationships are not about what is done for us, but about knowing and caring for other people.

Our relationships with others need to be on God's terms, not on theirs. Having a relationship with someone who is not relying on God can be an effort to meet needs that only God can meet. The only way to help them is to encourage their dependence on God, and to assist them in any way we can. A healthy relationship occurs when each person is depending on God and loving Him first. If people depend on us rather than on God, we need to point them to God and continue to have our needs met in Him.

Since we are all at different stages of spiritual growth and understanding, we need to have patience with one another. At times those that are hurting need to be heard, over and over again. Being able to share the pain they are in is part of the healing process. At what point do we call a halt to it? Before we "draw the line" we must pray; we must ask God for the wisdom that is needed in our actions and words. If someone does not want our biblical counsel, if they refuse to depend on God, it is necessary to withdraw support from them, even if this seems to be unkind. What is unkind is to allow them to depend on us, and not direct them to God. To be kind is to demonstrate the love of God to them by listening and reminding them of God's truth, love, goodness and faithfulness.

We may find that even if we love other people with the love of God, they may not be receptive. Being in a right relationship with God does not guarantee good relationships with others. Some may resent bringing God into the conversation because they want to live life on their terms. Even other believers may react this way. If the way we live and speak reflects our love for God, those who are disobedient are going to resent the contrast. We may be considered "politically incorrect!"

Regardless of whether we are accepted, rejected, liked or disliked, or have a personality clash or difference in opinion, we are commanded to love others. Just exactly what does this mean and what does it look like? How is it possible?

Loving Others

God provides guidelines for healthy relationships: to love God with our whole heart, soul, and mind and to love our neighbor as our self (Luke 10:27). The order given of loving God first, then our neighbor is not happenstance. Not only is God worthy of being loved first above all else, He is what makes it possible to love others sacrificially.

Other Scriptures define what love is (1 Corinthians 13) and further detail how that love is applied in relationships (Ephesians 4:29,32; 1 Peter 3; Romans 12:10). Not only does God enable us to love (for He is love), these passages describe what real love is so that we are not fooled by the world's false definitions of love.

Love always seeks what is good and best. 1 Corinthians 13, the well-known love chapter of the Bible describes the characteristics of love as: "patient, kind, not jealous, does not brag or boast, is not arrogant, does not seek its own, is not easily provoked, does not keep track of offenses, does not rejoice in evil, but in truth, bears all things, believes all things, hopes all things, endures all things, and never fails." Love's source is God; it is not motivated, supplied by anything that anyone does or is ("...love is of God..." 1 John 4: 7). Our source for loving others is spiritual (God is spirit, John 4:24); it is not emotional or physical. This does not mean that emotions are not involved; it simply means that they are not what motivate us or supply us with what we need. Emotional and physical feelings are dependent on stimuli for a response; they are reactionary. When God is our source, He motivates us to love with His love, which is consistent with His character. When God is our source of love, the expression of that love will not be determined by how people respond or by whether they deserve it or not, for as God is true and consistent, so is His love. We love, not for what people do or do not do, but because God first loved us (1 John 4:19), and He enables us to love.

Difficulties in our relationships usually stem from how love is expressed or applied. A big misconception is that love is doing what **feels** good. We are sure that we are "in love" for instance, because that person "makes us feel so good." How many times have we heard of someone who thought they were loved, but had been deceived, because they were told what they wanted to hear? They interpreted the other person's actions by how they felt, rather than by the Word of God.

True love, in contrast, is only concerned with a person's best interests, even if it includes pain. God's love has a two-fold goal: first, of deepening our love relationship with Him, and second, to conform us to the image of His Son. (The first is accomplished by the second). This was demonstrated when He sent His own beloved Son to die on the cross for our sin, so that a relationship with Him would be possible. God's demonstration of His love for us could not be a clearer example of doing that which is painful for the benefit of others. To love others is to demonstrate the love that God has demonstrated to us. Romans 12:9-21 tells us to "Let love be without hypocrisy … be kindly affectionate to one another … giving preference to one another … rejoice with those who rejoice, weep with those who weep." Love is demonstrated when we do what we say we are going to do, are kind and compassionate, and are willing to participate in the joy and sadness in other people's lives.

Scripture also states "whatever you want men to do to you, do also to them" (Matthew 7:12) and "love your neighbor as yourself" (Matthew 19:19). Matthew 7:12 does not mean using ourselves as the rule for conduct, or not doing what we consider is offensive. Instead, loving our neighbor is being concerned about them as much as we do ourselves. This is the essence of kindness, consideration and courtesy, and includes being aware of the culture and customs of the people we are interacting with. Loving others means going the extra mile, and perhaps following rules that we feel are unnecessary or illogical. It is being willing to recognize that love can be expressed in many ways, and that we need to try to express it in ways that the other person is going to understand.

The most difficult aspect of loving others is the command given in Matthew 5:44: "But I say to you, love your enemies, bless those who curse you, do good to those who hate you, and pray for those who spitefully use you and persecute you." It sounds good on paper, but when we have been despitefully used, persecuted, or emotionally or physically harmed by another person, loving them doesn't make sense. Bringing them to justice is what makes sense. But God's ways are not man's ways; the most Christ-like thing we can do is to show mercy and grace to someone who does not deserve it. (Did He not do the same for us?)

Love does not desire or seek retaliation. It does not hope for the offender to receive in kind what they have done to others. Romans 12: 18-20 states: "If it is possible, as much as depends on you, live peaceably with all men. Beloved, do not avenge yourselves, but rather give place to wrath, for it is written, 'Vengeance is Mine, I will repay,' says the Lord. Therefore 'If your enemy is hungry, feed him; If he is thirsty, give him a drink; for in so doing you will heap coals of fire on his head.'" Love earnestly desires to restore the one who is attacking or rebelling into fellowship with God and others. Love sees the damage that sinners do to themselves and to their relationship with

God; what they do to themselves and God is much worse than anything they do to us.

We are commanded to love our enemies and pray for them. I have found that it is hard to hate someone that I am praying for. How do we pray? First, ask God to help you see them through His eyes. God will enable us to forgive when we ask Him. Then pray for opportunities to demonstrate love to them. This could mean doing something that we don't like to do and helping when it is unexpected. Whenever there is an opportunity to be gracious, kind, helpful, forgiving, take it. The only reason this is even possible is because we have been forgiven a debt we could not pay; and we have the Holy Spirit who helps us do His Will. "We love Him, because He first loved us" (1 John 4:19).

In summary, loving others is: 1) considering the needs of others before our own: being willing to be inconvenienced and uncomfortable for their sake; 2) showing compassion, mercy, grace, and forgiveness; 3) taking the time to establish relationships with them; and 4) being willing to do what is in their best interest, even if it is painful for us or them. Loving others is not: 1) doing for others only when they do for us; 2) trying to do anything to change them (only God can); 3) trying to be God for them (seeking to fix them, or be everything for them).

Loving others biblically only happens if God abides in us (we abide in Him). Loving others has nothing to do with how they make us feel; it is a love that God gives us when we are in fellowship with Him. Love for others, then, is not based on anything another person says or does. True love from God can never be manipulated; it is always given freely. Loving others, then, means encouraging an ever-increasing sensitivity to sin and hatred of it, while at the same time encouraging an ever-increasing sensitivity to the Holy Spirit and love for God.

Why Am I So Miserable If This is the Lord's Will

False Expectations of Love

A hindrance in our relationships with others is the false expectation of what love is and how it is expressed. False expectations are unrealistic; it is to expect an expression of love from others that they are unaware of, unable, or unwilling to give. False expectations are based on an incorrect definition of what love is. When being loved is defined as having other people doing what we want them to do for us when and how we want them to do it, it is making our happiness contingent upon their behavior. This is the root of the problem. Some people want physical expressions, like a hug; others want tangible expressions, like a written note or flowers; others may want a verbal expression. When a certain expression is hoped for, and not received, disappointment follows. **Disappointment should be expected when our expectations become demands**; it can also be expected because only God can love us perfectly. We cannot expect other people to love us as only God can. Even if a person loves others with God's love, their expression of that love is going to be limited.

Understanding the limitations that are present in each one of us is vital to a correct expectation of love from others and how love is to be expressed. Since God created us to have relationships, it is a God-given desire to want to connect with others. But we are limited: we cannot know other people as only God knows them; we cannot always be there when we are needed; we are limited by time, responsibilities, and our sinful natures. Because of these limitations, losses of communication take place, either in not communicating what is wrong or what is needed, or in not saying what should be said. Is it any wonder that there are so many misunderstandings and hurt feelings in relationships?

Do our limitations mean that we should not expect anything from others? Does our behavior not matter? How we treat each other certainly does matter; otherwise, God would not have commanded us to love one another, be kind, compassionate, truthful, and so forth. How do we respond, then, when we don't feel loved? Our first response should always be to go to the Lord. Is the communication line open with Him? Is there any sin blocking fellowship? If not, then it may be due to a limitation in us or them.

We may feel unloved because of a personal attack. When someone **feels** threatened, that is all that is required for an attack. Why do people attack? To protect or promote themselves. They are not trusting God to take care of them; they seek to provide for their own needs in their own strength. They do not submit to God, but follow their own will and demand their own way. This alienates them from God and leads to personal misery. If I forgive when I am attacked, I demonstrate God's love. Even if they do not respond to this forgiveness, God is our help, strength, and healing, and we are actually much better off than the one who is attacking us, even if it looks as though they are getting away with it.

To correct a false expectation of love, we need to find our source of happiness and well-being in the Lord and base our expectations of loving behavior on the Word of God. When we no longer rely on other people to make us happy, we are then more concerned about their behavior as it relates to God rather than how it affects us.

Acceptance from Others

We all have the desire to be accepted by others, for God created us to be relational to Him and others. But since the Fall (Genesis 3), the desire for relationships with others has replaced having a relationship with God. As a result, our sense of worth and value is not found in God, but in how we are received and treated by others. To be accepted by others is not just something nice and enjoyable; it is a matter of survival. Not having friends or being rejected by others is what is most feared. Those who do not have friends find themselves on the outside looking in. Such a situation is deplorable and miserable, and can result in becoming suicidal.

No matter the talents, abilities, or physical beauty we have, we all feel inadequate about something. When we are honest with ourselves, we are afraid that if our faults, weaknesses, failings, sins, or differences were known, we would be rejected. Since we crave acceptance, understanding, and validation from others, we try to behave in a way in which our differences and failings are not apparent. This does not really give us what we are looking for. There is no real understanding or validation for who we really are and what we stand for because so much of us is hidden. This creates a dilemma; we can reveal what we really are and what we believe, and risk being rejected; or we can present what we think other people want to see, and we will feel accepted, but they won't know us.

The risk of being rejected by others is real. It does and will happen. We think that if we do the right thing, that we will be liked and accepted. So acceptance is sought by earning it. If I say the right things, perform well, do things for them, give them gifts, maybe they will like me. People will respond to these things; the problem is that this acceptance is always based on what we do for them, not on who we are. Acceptance from others, then, cannot be earned. Doing well does not only earn acceptance, it can result in resentment and manipulation. God's love, however, accepts a person as they are, and is not based on physical appearance, achievements, or personality. "But God demonstrates His own love toward us, in that while we were still sinners, Christ died for us" (Romans 5:8).

When we are rejected because we don't "fit in," we look for a group that will accept us. This results in a social clique; a set group is formed that is comfortable with its size and with the people it knows. The group associates only with those who make them feel accepted. There is no real acceptance; they just feel comfortable with the activities they like to do in common. Because being accepted is desired, the group member ends up doing to others outside the group what they originally hoped to eliminate for themselves: rejection.

All this shows that trying to find the basis of our acceptance, value and worth in our relationships with others will not work. The significance and priority we place on those relationships is wrong. We were created to have a relationship with God and when this is our first priority, His word, His opinion, His love, His approval matter the most. Ephesians 1:5-7 makes clear the basis of our acceptance: "Having predestinated us unto the adoption of children by Jesus Christ to himself, according to the good pleasure of His will, to the praise of the glory of His grace, wherein *He hath made us accepted in the beloved.* In whom we have redemption through His blood, the forgiveness of sins, according to the riches of His grace." (Italics mine)

Only God gives real acceptance, validation, understanding, and solace in what He has provided through His son. We need to find our place, meet our need for connection, that sense of belonging in the Lord. Only God knows and understands us. We will not find completion in anyone else. We were designed for our Creator. No one understands us better than the One Who created us. No one loves us better than God, who sent His Son to die for us, or the Son, who did die for us, or the Spirit, who indwells us. There is no greater acceptance found than what is found in God through Christ Jesus.

Our sin has separated us from God; there is nothing **we** can do that will make us acceptable. Only the blood of Jesus Christ covers our transgressions and makes acceptance possible. "While we were yet sinners, Christ died for us" (Romans 5:8). Our confidence is not based on our abilities or accomplishments, but on the righteousness of Christ. God has made acceptance possible through the death of His Son. All we need to do is come to Him, admitting our need of His forgiveness, love, healing, and strength. Our acceptance by God is secure because He Himself has made it sure.

We are accepted by God! He is our Creator who loves us perfectly and who has made our salvation and sanctification possible. But just because we know we are accepted by God does not mean that we will not experience rejection from people. We may cause offense in some way, and rejection will result. Are we complainers? Are we always negative and critical? Are we self-centered or self-righteous? Do we always insist on our way?

It may also be true that what we **perceive** as rejection may not actually be rejection. People can be so busy that they are unaware that their lack of interaction is being interpreted as rejection. This is when we need to have a forgiving spirit. "Be ye kind one to another, forgiving one another, even as God for Christ's sake has forgiven you" (Ephesians 4:32). But it can also be true that we may experience what we consider rude and self-centered behavior. People may simply be modeling what they have seen and known, or their behavior may be a result of environment and abuse or a lack of ability and knowledge. Those who are introverted or lack social ability may not have a clue that they are offending anyone. Never assume the offense is intentional, unless it is specifically stated as such. If we are offended, Matthew 18:15-20 instructs us to go to our brother/sister. Ask if they understand how their behavior is affecting others. Their behavior can only change after being made aware of the problem, and then depending on God to change them.

What about people we find difficult to accept? We are all created by God and need to be respected on that basis alone. Asking God to help us see them through His eyes can change our attitude toward them. Finding acceptance in God frees us to be all He created us to be. This enables us to accept other people, even when they do not accept us. God tells us in His Word to bear one another's burdens, and Christian fellowship, when it is all it can be, is the sweetest fellowship that can be found on earth.

Pursuing acceptance from others is a futile exercise. What is acceptable in some circumstances is not acceptable in others. But while what is acceptable is always changing, and sometimes unattainable, God's acceptance **never** changes. If we rest in the acceptance that God has provided, we will find the peace, protection, healing, and strength that we need to pursue relationships with others.

Manipulation

But Jesus called them to Himself and said, "You know that the rulers of the Gentiles lord it over them, and those who are great exercise authority over them. Yet it shall not be so among you; but whoever desires to become great among you, let him be your servant. (Matthew 20:25-26)

To be manipulated is to be coerced into doing or not doing something by either physical or emotional means. Most of the time this manipulation is emotional: either fear of rejection, loss of love and acceptance, or guilt, whether it is done by family or peers. We can be so used to being manipulated that we do not even recognize when it happens. People pleasers are the most often manipulated, for they will often do what they don't want to do to please others.

But whether we want to admit it or not, we have all been manipulated, and we all try to manipulate to get things the way we want them. To get other people to do what we want brings a sense of power and control; it also feeds self-righteousness, for the more people we can manipulate, the more we are empowered to feel that our way is right. Even if we claim that we are following God's way, if our intent is to have our own way and get other people to do it, we have established ourselves as the standard by which to live. This, more than the resentment that comes from being manipulated, is what is so abhorrent about manipulation. It is directly opposed to humble submission to God's will, God's way, or God's rule.

What do we do when we know someone is trying to manipulate us and we are being made to feel as though we have no choice? If we feel we are

Why Am I So Miserable If This is the Lord's Will

forced into doing something, we can choose what our attitude will be and seek to honor God.

Manipulation cannot be avoided. Even though I may be able to recognize manipulative behavior a mile away, there will always be someone out there who knows how to "push my buttons." Telling ourselves that we aren't going to be manipulated doesn't work. The secret to dealing with manipulation is not to **avoid** it, but to **submit** to the Spirit's control. When we choose to respond God's way, no matter how someone else is making us feel, they are not in control; God is.

Some people will be successful in manipulating our emotions; but this will have no permanent effect on us if we choose to forgive. We can forgive because we are forgiven. With God's help and enablement, we can choose to do what they ask, if it is right; or, we can refuse, knowing that God will help us through the fallout of that choice.

Doing what the manipulator asks may appear as though we are letting them control us. God knows our hearts; we cannot convince the manipulator of the reasons for our capitulation. They choose to believe only what supports their behavior, and any protest falls on deaf ears. The benefit in choosing to do what is right is not in "keeping the peace" or from inwardly thwarting their efforts (standing up on the inside when we are sitting down outwardly). Any true benefit comes from the peace that God gives that passes all understanding, knowing that what we do is for Him, and that what other people intend for evil, God uses for good (Genesis 50:20).

Saying no to manipulators can be really tough, whether confronting is difficult for us or not. Often the people who manipulate us the most are the ones we are closest to and care for the most. It is because we care that we are emotionally vulnerable. But even if the person we care about the most rejects us because we would not do what they wanted, God more than supplies any need we have for comfort and healing. Anytime we respond in obedience to His Word at personal cost to ourselves, we are blessed: "Blessed are they which are persecuted for righteousness' sake: for theirs is the kingdom of heaven" (Matthew 5:10).

How do we choose to do something that we don't want to do? Only by doing it out of love for the other person.

For you, brethren, have been called to liberty; only do not use liberty as an opportunity for the flesh, but through love serve one another. For all the law is fulfilled in one word, even in this: 'You shall love your neighbor as yourself.' (Galatians 5:13-14)

Serving is not a burden if we choose to serve the Lord with our whole heart. But, when we do something out of a sense of obligation or duty, or "because we have to," it becomes a burden. We have the choice to either live our lives in aggravation, depression, boredom, (etc.) or, we can decide beforehand to be God's servant, depending on Him to enable us to do whatever needs to be done. We may not always like what we are doing, but the task is always easier if we do it with a willing heart.

I am not implying here that we should be willing to do anything someone else wants; it does not mean allowing abuse or giving the flesh an opportunity to be a "martyr," taking on more than we can accomplish, or suffering for personal glory. When our motive is to glorify God it will be demonstrated by our love for Him and others. Loving others may mean being willing to be unpopular, because we will want to do what is best for them rather than what they want. Rejection is always a possibility. Though being rejected hurts, what we need is to choose between pleasing man and pleasing God (1 Peter 5:7; Philippians 4:19).

Conflict with Others

...for you are still carnal. For where there are envy, strife, and divisions among you, are you not carnal and behaving like mere men? (1 Corinthians 3:3)

Conflict with other people occurs for any number of reasons, and the causes of conflict are the same with everyone, regardless of how conflict is manifested. Some of those reasons are: 1) unrealistic or unreasonable expectations; 2) judging others by personal and not Biblical standards; 3) self-interest; and 4) assumptions. These reasons are expanded below.

1. One of the most common reasons for stress in our relationships is unrealistic or unreasonable expectations; whether we intend to have expectations or not, we have them. The question is: what expectations are right, and what expectations are unrealistic or unreasonable?

   There are expectations of others that are correct, depending on whether they walk in darkness or walk in the light. 1 John 2:9-11 states: "He who says he is in the light, and hates his brother, is in darkness until now. He who loves his brother abides in the light, and there is no cause for stumbling in him. But he who hates his brother is in darkness and walks in darkness, and does not know where he is going, because the darkness has blinded his eyes." Galatians 5: 19-25 describes characteristics of the Flesh (darkness) and the Spirit (light):

   "Now the works of the flesh are evident, which are: adultery, fornication, uncleanness, lewdness, idolatry, sorcery, hatred, contentions, jealousies, outbursts of wrath, selfish ambitions, dissensions, heresies, envy, murders, drunkenness, revelries, and

the like; of which I tell you beforehand, just as I also told you in time past, that those who practice such things will not inherit the kingdom of God. But the fruit of the Spirit is love, joy, peace, longsuffering, kindness, goodness, faithfulness, gentleness, self-control. Against such there is no law. And those who are Christ's have crucified the flesh with its passions and desires. If we live in the Spirit, let us also walk in the Spirit."

Scripture makes a clear distinction between behaviors that are of God and behaviors that are of the flesh or darkness or sin. We can expect self-centered, self-protective, prideful and unloving behavior from people who don't obey God. Those in fellowship with God will demonstrate the fruit of the Spirit. Even if what people do appears to be good, if they have rejected God and His Word, their "good" behavior is rooted in selfish motives. If we are working with those who have not submitted to Jesus Christ, we need not be surprised when they act according to their fleshly nature. If someone claims to be a believer, but does not act like it, our expectations will lead to disappointment, for those who love God and know God will have some evidence in their behavior. When Christians do not act like the children of God that they are, it means that they are not walking in the Spirit, but walking according to the flesh.

Unrealistic or unreasonable expectations happen when we expect others to do things as we would do them, or without being told to do them, or to do something that is beyond their ability. It is not unrealistic to expect another believer to be seeking after God, or to have a goal of loving Him or others more. It is unrealistic to expect behavior of other believers that God does not expect from His children.

When is an expectation unreasonable? When we expect other people to meet needs that only God can meet; i.e., to be available when we

Why Am I So Miserable If This is the Lord's Will

need them, to do the things that we want them to do, to do them the way we want them done. An unreasonable expectation, by its very definition, is self-centered.

2. Being judgmental can also cause conflict. Those who are self-righteous judge others unfairly or improperly, either by judging motives or behavior by their own standards. Judging others is God's role: "But why do you judge your brother? Or why do you show contempt for your brother? For we shall all stand before the judgment seat of Christ" (Romans 14:10). But God's Word also teaches that believers are to discern between right and wrong.

Dare any of you, having a matter against another, go to law before the unrighteous, and not before the saints? Do you not know that the saints will judge the world? And if the world will be judged by you, are you unworthy to judge the smallest matters? Do you not know that we shall judge angels? How much more, things that pertain to this life? (1 Corinthians 6:1-3).

Judging properly means using the Word of God to evaluate conduct and confronting the conduct (in love) if it is contrary to the Word of God. Those who judge improperly impose standards that are not in the Word of God, or confront someone in sin, but without love. They love what is "right" more than God or others. Before confronting another's sin, we must first confront ourselves and make sure our sins have been confessed and determine our motives. We are to focus not on their fault, but on their need, praying and trusting that we can be God's instrument in meeting that need.

3. Another of the major causes for conflict is selfishness. This is seen in those who are unwilling to do anything outside of their comfort zone

for the sake of others. They disregard how their actions impact other people. If they are lazy, or sloppy, or rude, what does it matter? It does not bother them, so why should it bother anyone else? They live by their own rules, and everyone else needs to adjust to them.

Selfish people can also be opinionated. They will pick and choose from the Bible what they consider worth obeying and anyone questioning their choices is being "judgmental." Those who are selfish need to see how their behavior is affecting other people and learn that we are all accountable to God for our behavior.

4. Last, but not least, is making assumptions. The danger of making assumptions is that we draw conclusions based on inadequate information. Assumptions are made based on what we know and what we have experienced. Even if only one of our assumptions is wrong, our conclusion will be wrong. How many arguments, disagreements, and conflicts have arisen because of an assumption that someone has made? To avoid the conflict that arises from assumptions, we need to make sure we understand what the other person is trying to communicate, and make sure that we are understood. "And just as you want men to do to you, you also do to them likewise" (Luke 6:31).

If there is an overall cause for conflict, it is a lack of love for others. It is either love that we lack for them, or love that they lack for us. Even when we love someone as we ought, conflict may result from someone attacking us unjustly or for no apparent cause; it may also involve a person in sin who will not repent. Conflict cannot always be resolved. We cannot make other people repent, change, love, or grow in Christ. If a person refuses to live in submission to God, this always limits their relationship with others. When this happens, all we can do is to love them and pray for them. Loving them does not mean continuing in fellowship with them if they refuse to repent.

Doing so contradicts Matthew 18:15-20, when Jesus instructed his disciples on forgiveness:

> *"Moreover if your brother sins against you, go and tell him his fault between you and him alone. If he hears you, you have gained your brother. But if he will not hear, take with you one or two more, that 'by the mouth of two or three witnesses every word may be established.' And if he refuses to hear them, tell it to the church. But if he refuses even to hear the church, let him be to you like a heathen and a tax collector. Assuredly, I say to you, whatever you bind on earth will be bound in heaven, and whatever you loose on earth will be loosed in heaven. Again I say to you that if two of you agree on earth concerning anything that they ask, it will be done for them by My Father in heaven. For where two or three are gathered together in My name, I am there in the midst of them."*

Luke 17:3b-4 says: "If your brother sins against you, rebuke him; and if he repents, forgive him. And if he sins against you seven times in a day, and seven times in a day returns to you, saying, 'I repent,' you shall forgive him." Note that forgiveness occurs after repentance. I John 1:9 states that "If we confess our sins, He is faithful and just to forgive." We can only receive forgiveness of our sin if we acknowledge it and repent.

While forgiveness cannot be received unless there is repentance, it does not follow that we do not forgive others if there is no repentance. We are to "be kind to one another, tenderhearted, forgiving one other; even as God in Christ forgave you" (Ephesians 4:32); "not returning evil for evil or reviling for reviling, but on the contrary blessing…" (1 Peter 3:9). If someone has sinned against us and we have confronted them and rebuked them as Matthew

18 instructs and they have not repented, we are still to forgive them. But even if we are not continuing in fellowship with them, we can be kind. Being kind involves any encouragement we can give them to return to the Lord and to assure them of our love for them. Even if our relationship is never restored due to a lack of repentance, forgiving them honors God and frees us from the bondage of resentment, anger, and bitterness. "God has not given us a spirit of fear, but of power, of love, and a strong mind" (2 Timothy 1:7). We cannot love someone and hate them at the same time. The only way we can love someone who has hurt us is with the love that God makes available to us. We can forgive because we have received His forgiveness.

There will be times when people will avoid confrontation, arguments, disagreements and grievances by not saying anything or avoiding the person they are in conflict with. Their thinking is that denying there is a conflict — "keeping the peace"—is the Christian thing to do. Avoiding conflict will result in "not making waves;" but it will also result in artificial relationships. There will be no Christian fellowship.

Conflict may also be avoided because of an incorrect assumption: "they should have known," or "they know what they did." Conflict is seen as being pointless, assuming that they are well aware of their sin and are not repenting of it. This only justifies disobedience. Sharing the Word of God with unbelievers may result in rejection, conflict, or persecution, but this may also happen when sharing truth from God's Word with believers. Our friendships with other believers are important to us, and we may want to avoid anything that threatens to break up those relationships. Not wanting to lose a friend, not wanting to make waves, not thinking it is worth making a fuss over, are all reasons used for avoiding conflict.

Conflict is avoided because it is painful for us and for the other person. However, avoiding conflict simply because it is painful or difficult is selfish and unloving, caring more about ourselves than for them. To leave them in their sin does them greater harm than confronting them.

A good friend will challenge us to draw closer to God and will not be afraid to confront our sin and/or a blind spot. There is no question that more likely than not there will be fallout when sin is confronted. Believers have been known to absolutely deny sin; or, if it is acknowledged, deny any responsibility. Some have separated from fellowship altogether. Others continue to attend church as if nothing happened. But some do respond. Praise God.

Confrontation is sometimes necessary, but not enjoyed, especially if the one sinning does not repent. God does not guarantee that the one who sins will repent. Forgiving our brother does not mean restoration either. While we may forgive him, if he does not recognize his sin, he will not want our forgiveness (because he thinks he doesn't need it). A rift will continue to exist. Forgiveness is not pretending that there was no wrong. Forgiveness sees what was done wrong, but does not hold it against the person. The only reason we can forgive the most heinous of actions is because God has forgiven us and enables us to forgive. The unfortunate reality is that forgiving does not always result in restored relationships.

The worst thing that can happen is not that we lose all our friends, but that our fellowship with God is broken. It is our relationship with Him that sustains us whether our relationships with others are broken or not. The purpose of our relationships with others is not to increase our dependence on each other, but on God.

What if there is a conflict because someone believes or proclaims error? How is this properly evaluated and handled? Psalm 19:12 states: "Who can understand his errors? Cleanse me from secret faults." The root of error is always in the heart. "…Out of the abundance of the heart the mouth speaks" (Matthew 12:34; Luke 6:45). God's Word is the only standard for truth and for determining error; only His Spirit knows the heart and can judge it.

We may be able to show someone their error by expounding the Scriptures; they may seem to agree with what we are saying. However, it may just be passive-aggressive behavior. Instead of disagreeing with us, they say what they think we want to hear. The only way we can know for sure is by a change in their behavior. Are they continuing to live for themselves, or for God?

The purpose of confrontation is always to restore the sinner. If we truly love others, we will be more concerned with the damage that their sin is doing to their relationship with God than we are concerned about whatever offense is being done against us.

We always have to be aware that Scripture says "he that is spiritual" is to go to his brother; in other words we must not confront if we are out of fellowship with God ourselves.

Conflict resolution isn't about righting wrong or proving or being proven wrong; it is about understanding the damage sin does to our relationship with God, to ourselves, as well as to other people in our lives. It is about helping them to recognize that our real enemy is sin, and learning how destructive it is in our lives, and trusting God to deliver them from it.

When We Get Hurt

Let no corrupt word proceed out of your mouth, but what is good for necessary edification, that it may impart grace to the hearers ... and be kind to one another, tenderhearted, forgiving one another, even as God in Christ forgave you. (Ephesians 4:29,32)

Love suffers long and is kind; ...does not seek its own, is not provoked, thinks no evil; does not rejoice in iniquity, but rejoices in the truth; bears all things, believes all things, hopes all things, endures all things ...(1 Corinthians 13: 4-7a)

Why Am I So Miserable If This is the Lord's Will

We all are sensitive (whether we realize it or not) and may be hurt from a slight, insult, ridicule, or out-right rejection. What differs from person to person is how we react at the moment and what we do with the hurt afterward. There are two possible reactions: to "toughen up" or to become hypersensitive and demanding.

Even if we forgive the people who hurt us, we can let fear of people hurting us again cause us to ignore any hurt feelings, not giving them any credence—not revealing any vulnerability or weakness that someone else can take advantage of. This is "toughening up." When we are tough, nothing but the most in-your-face attack appears to bother us. But in stamping down the hurt we feel from small hurts, we are in effect agreeing with the person who hurt us. By belittling the hurt, we belittle ourselves, which is directly opposite of God's view that each of us is valued because we are created in His image.

When we toughen ourselves, we lack compassion for other people. This is not a conscious thought; it is a reaction that happens when we hear or see someone complaining about something we wouldn't give a second thought to. If they are offended by what we said or did, we do not think we are at fault —they are at fault because they need to "grow up" or "get over it." Since in toughening up we have lost some of our sensitivity, their reaction looks like an over-reaction; because we are hard on ourselves, we are just as hard on others.

The flip side of the coin is those who never toughen up, but have become even more sensitive with each hurt, and subsequently complain all the time and demand redress for every perceived injury, whether it is real or not. They can be so vigilant in addressing slights and hurts that they will see them when none was intended. For them, any hurt, real or perceived, is blown out of proportion. Being hurt is so feared that any situation in which they might be hurt is avoided. Many people avoid the hypersensitive person, not because they do not care, but because they do not know what is going to offend them.

This becomes a self-fulfilling prophecy: hyper-sensitive people believe no one likes them, and then end up behaving in such a way as to be unlikeable.

Although they will claim to be more sensitive and caring than the tough person, too often they are so busy feeling sorry for themselves and seeking redress for the latest injury that they either do not see the needs of others or do not consider them as important as their needs at the moment. Right and wrong is not determined by the Word of God, but by how what is said or done affects them.

Neither approach deals with pain nor hurt properly. To belittle hurts does not lessen it or the damage it does; to obsess over hurts only exasperates, intensifies, and prolongs the hurt. No matter which way the flesh seeks to handle the injuries we receive, it will fail us. It is not going to heal us, and it is going to disable our relationships with others. The first inclination of the flesh is to hurt the other person. Why do we want to see others suffer? The obvious answer is vengeance; but it goes deeper than that. We want other people to suffer in the same way we have because we want to feel justified for feeling sorry for ourselves. Not only that, but if we see them experiencing the same thing we have but not handling it as well as we did, that bolsters our pride and self-sufficiency. While we are bemoaning the pain of an injury, dealing with this injury in the flesh is to commit an even greater offense against God.

Everyone has experienced hurt; and everyone feels sorry for themselves. When we are really hurt, that hurt can feel immense; when other people don't acknowledge how bad it is for us, the pity party begins. The flesh always seeks to justify its sin, whether it is a lack of forgiveness, self-pity, pride, or self-sufficiency. We like to see ourselves as the victim. We genuinely think and feel that no one has gone through what we have, and if they did, they certainly had more support than we did. Our refusal to walk in the Spirit, according to the Word of God is based on the rationalization that if we had had it better, if we had been treated right, if God cared more, etc., then our hurt would've been healed by now. Since it hasn't, well, who can blame us for the grudge we bear, or the chip on our shoulder?

The flesh rationalizes either our lack of forgiveness or lack of love proportionally to the amount of pain and hurt that we feel from the injury we receive. How easy it is to condemn the person(s) who injure us, yet not take our own sin seriously! But there can be **no** healing until we repent of our own sin. Only then is our fellowship with God restored, and God can begin to heal the hurt.

To not forgive is sin; there is **no** pain that justifies sin. Any means by which the flesh seeks to justify its action is pointless. The only way we will honor God is to ask Him for strength and help to forgive the offender, to repent of the sin we have committed against Him in our response to the injury, and to pray for more love for others. We need God's perspective on the situation, so that we can see the injury for what it is. Then, to follow the commands of Scripture, going to our brother and communicating the offense (Matthew 18:15-18), and forgiving whether there is an apology or not (Ephesians 4:32). An important part of forgiving is putting the hurt in God's hands and leaving it there; **this is only possible with God's strength.**

If we have forgiven someone, yet the old hurt keeps resurfacing, it may be that we are dwelling on old injuries. We like to think that if we could just understand this, then we will be healed; or if we can get enough people to commiserate with us, then we will be healed. This feels good to the flesh, but it does not bring healing. If people had treated us more kindly, that certainly would make life easier, but it does not resolve the problem of our injuries. Better circumstances and nicer people may make us feel better momentarily, but they cannot and do not make us better. They only enable self-pity and self-reliance! God alone brings healing. To argue with, reason with, bargain with our flesh will only result in bondage to the flesh—we are stuck in the "slough of despond."[21] Our flesh is a master of self-justification and rationalization.

What then can we do? Healing cannot take place until we surrender the injury over to God **continually**. In Romans 12:1 Paul urges us to be a "living sacrifice." It is not a one-time event. The flesh and its deeds have to be put to death daily. It is not making an effort to remember the injury just to surrender it to God, but to recognize how the flesh is leading us down the path of self-pity, vengeance, pride, and then to repent of it. When seeking to be healed by God we cannot love others if our hurt or injuries are all we think about. Obsessing about the past only feeds the flesh and heads down the road of self-pity. A lack of forgiveness is characterized by anger and bitterness; and to keep remembering the injury is a device of the flesh and Satan. The flesh wants us to feel sorry for ourselves, dwell on the injury and play the victim.

The only right way of dealing with hurts is to see it from God's perspective. If we have forgiven, yet we struggle with the lingering pain of the injury, we must actively trust God to take care of us and heal us as we pray for His strength. When we are hurt, we must find out first if an offense was intended. If it was not intended, we have to find out what was intended. This is not to belittle the hurt we received, but to help us alter our perceptions and expectations of other people's behavior. We are not the center of the universe! God is! And He is the only One who deserves to be. For any injury that we are struggling with we can also receive support from godly people who will pray with us.

Husbands & Wives

Husbands, love your wives, just as Christ also loved the church and gave Himself for her ... (Ephesians 5:25)

Wives, submit to your own husbands, as is fitting in the Lord. (Colossians 3:18)

Why Am I So Miserable If This is the Lord's Will

What was man created for? What was woman created for? The answers to these questions are fundamental to our understanding of what relationships between men and women were meant to be like.

Genesis 1:27 tells us "So God created man in His own image; in the image of God He created him; male and female He created them." Out of all the creatures that God made, man (and woman) were the only ones made in His image. Genesis 1-3 does not record God pursuing fellowship with any of the other creatures He made. Both man and woman were created to be distinct from the rest of creation and to rule over it (Genesis 1:28) and to have fellowship with God contingent upon obedience and trust in His word and command.

For what purpose was woman created? She was created to be a helper suitable for Adam (Genesis 2), created for man, from man. When Eve was deceived and sinned and Adam chose to sin, it brought death: spiritual, emotional, relational, and physical. While we have a tendency to emphasize the consequence of physical death, the spiritual death that resulted was even more devastating and spiritual life after that was possible only by the grace of God. Sin required a sacrifice, a covering in order for there to be fellowship with God. The Old Testament sacrificial system instituted by God (the book of Leviticus gives this in detail) looked forward to the promised Messiah; New Testament believers look back to the sacrifice of Christ as payment for their sin (Isaiah 53).

God provided a means for dealing with sin: repentance, and covering (sacrifice) for sin. Our relationship with Him is restored when we repent and receive forgiveness. Sin (the fleshly sin nature we inherit from the Fall) causes relationship problems.

The curse that was put on Adam and Eve after the Fall affects relationships. For the woman: "your desire shall be for your husband, and he shall rule over you" (Genesis 3:16); man's curse: hard toil and labor to provide for his family. Note that these are curses! The Fall turned woman's focus off of God to men; it turned man's focus from God to work.

Before the Fall, women didn't have any pain in childbirth; her desire would not be focused on her husband (either making him God or seeking to rule over him), but would be for God. Her delight would be in serving Him by being the helper for her husband. But there was a Fall, and as a result, women's fleshly desires are fixated on men. The curse can also be seen in the desperation of many women to get married and to look to their husbands to meet their needs and make them happy. But that isn't what God created women for, and it isn't what God created men for. Women were created to be complete in God, not in a man; men were not created to fulfill or complete women.

It is God that fulfills and completes us. To put marriage or our husband in God's place will only lead to conflict, frustration, and disappointment. When our needs are met in God, we are then freed from this frustration. Serving our husband is not done out of duty or resentment, or to get something in return; it is done with joy and with the hope that our service will assist him in his walk, work, or ministry.

It is tragic when a woman exalts herself above the place God intended for her. Instead of using her gifts to be the helpmeet for her husband, she takes over his position through criticism, disapproval, and condescension. The flesh would always have us believe that we must take matters into our own hands if things are going to get done and if our needs are going to be met. So we try to get our husbands or other people to give us what we want and need. The flesh always wants immediate resolution! God's way will never make sense to the flesh. "Serve our husbands! I bet they'll like that!" To our way of thinking, that would only result in getting less of what we want and need. How can that be any good?

But it isn't God that is nonsensical; it is the flesh. For what it tells us we must pursue to get what we want or need will always ultimately fail. God's way is to find what we need in Him, which then frees us to be the helpers He created us to be. Women will find the most satisfaction when they enable and support their husband in what he needs to do. To live a life devoted to pleasing ourselves, or idolizing or controlling men, is to be miserable. The curse of sin is such that we can be convinced that **not** doing things God's way is the only way to be happy; the opposite is true. When a woman fears the LORD, and understands the purpose(s) for which women were created, she is then freed to be what she is meant to be; with the result of joy, contentment, and peace for her, and a blessing for every life she comes in contact with, in particular her family (Proverbs 31).

Before the Fall, man wasn't so compelled to work; his sense of purpose did not come from his occupation, but from his relationship with God. Before the curse on creation, His work and relationships were satisfying. He would not rule over his wife, but would instead love her and seek to worship and serve God with her.

But there is a curse on man from the Fall, and the result is men that look to everything but God for their identity, manhood, purpose, and validation. They will look to status, achievement, control, power, wealth, or possessions for these things, yet what they pursue eludes them. How many men have poured their lives into a certain pursuit for 20 or 30 years, and then realized that what they have achieved doesn't matter, and in the process they have neglected their relationship with God and others, which is the only thing that does matter?

Not only are their relationships neglected in this pursuit, other people are put down, controlled or manipulated when what they do fails them. How is this seen in marriage? It is seen in avoidance of responsibility and communication or in personal attacks. Our flesh rebels against any role that God has placed us in, whether it is the submissive role of the wife or the role of headship given to man; as a result, the natural desire of men is to avoid any responsibility for decisions in the home. "Blame games" take place as responsibility is avoided. If a wife criticizes her husband for lack of leadership, involvement, or decision-making, he then attacks her.

This was never what God intended for marriage! When a man will accept the role that God has given him, and approach that role humbly and with love, only then will he find the fulfillment and purpose that he was both looking for and created for.

Women should not expect men to be like women; men should not expect women to behave like men, or have low regard for their emotions. Both women and men were created by God to be distinctly different from one another. Judging, rejecting, criticizing, and disapproving each other will destroy relationships and couples miss out on God's blessings.

What a good marriage is NOT: having our husband there when and where we want him, doing or saying what we want and need him to say; or having our wife be our maid, mother, or sex slave. When the focus for either the husband or wife is on themselves, and on what they want or need, the marriage will fail. To expect someone to meet all our needs is to set ourselves up for disappointment. A marriage is not about someone else making us happy; neither is it finding someone who completes us. The only thing that completes us is our relationship with God.

It is also important to realize that marriage is not a remedy for lust. While it does provide a God-honoring outlet for sex within marriage, a problem with lust before marriage is not going to go away just because you are married. Sexual lust, just like any other lust of the flesh, is defeated the same way in or out of marriage: by walking in and according to the Spirit, and turning away from those lusts and turning to the Lord. To think that our lust can be controlled or will be contained by marriage is wrong; also, to see marriage as a place where lust can be indulged or carried to extremes is to see our partner not as a person, but as a sexual object. Any such treatment will ultimately destroy marriages.

Why Am I So Miserable If This is the Lord's Will

What a good marriage IS: each accepting each other's limitations, loving and forgiving each other with God's love, which comes from a good relationship with Him. A good marriage has God at its center. When a marriage is firmly rooted and established in Him, it will thrive, grow, and remain. When both man and wife each find their joy, peace, satisfaction and contentment in God, their chief delight will be in sharing their walk with God with each other and assisting each other to draw closer to Him. The closer we draw to God, the more we will desire not to live life for ourselves; marriage will be seen as an adventure in self-denial. A good relationship between husband and wife is not a mutual demand for needs to be met; it is putting aside our needs for the sake of the other, while depending on God to meet our needs.

Loving each other with God's love is seen when the offended partner does not blame the other for not meeting actual or perceived needs, and repents of any bitterness or anger toward the other. This will not happen if there is any sin in their life that is blocking fellowship with God. That is why keeping in constant fellowship with God is essential for a healthy marriage. If only one is in a right relationship with God, the marriage may not fail (due to the faithfulness of the one) but there will be no mutual fellowship in Christ. I have unfortunately seen several marriages like this; some with unsaved partners, others with a partner who is saved, but who does not appear to be growing in Christ. These marriages can be very difficult and discouraging; but again, if hope, strength, and love are found in God, divorce need not be considered. Even if circumstances never change, God will minister in and through that situation way beyond our expectations when we submit to His will as we trust and depend on Him.

As each person is different, and will have different means of coping with the stresses of life, we can expect that whomever we marry will have coping mechanisms that differ from ours. This means that the way our husband or wife copes may actually cause us stress, and vice versa. We realize that there will be problems encountered in marriage—but we may not expect that the way we cope with life is what causes conflict with others. Two examples of conflicting coping mechanisms are: a person who has to have cleanliness and order to cope marries someone who gets stressed out if they are not surrounded by clutter; or a person who thrives on being with people marries someone who thrives on being able to spend some time alone. No matter what it is that our flesh tries to convince us of that we have to have to cope, we can cope without out it if we depend on God for what we need. When we don't depend on God, but demand that our husband/wife facilitate what our flesh is demanding, it will cause conflict and frustration. If we expect a marriage to be healthy and successful, we must die to the flesh and its demands.

No matter how well we cope, we can be sure that the ways of the flesh always destroy relationships! Our coping mechanisms are diabolical; while they appear to be benign and necessary, they are in fact self-serving. Rather than being harmless, they do immeasurable harm to us, to our relationship with God and our relationship with others. The more the flesh seeks to protect and serve itself, the more damage is done, for any attempt at self-protection or self-provision will always have a negative impact on others. We protect ourselves either by shutting other people out, or by attacking; self-provision puts taking care of ourselves before anyone else, and results in being demanding or neglectful of others. Anything that the flesh demands is always self-centered. "So what is the big deal if I am self-centered, as long as I don't do anything to hurt someone?" is like asking "What's wrong with wallowing in the mud, as long as I don't get dirty?" We cannot be self-centered and not hurt others, no matter how much we white-wash our motives. Though selfish motives can be hidden for awhile, true motives will always come to light when our flesh's comfort is tested. When selfishness is revealed, it alienates others and disables relationships. The only way for a marriage to be all that it can be is for it to be centered on and dependent upon God.

Those who are married will experience the problems that a fleshly nature brings to the relationship. Instead of focusing on what husbands or wives are or aren't doing, we need to forgive one another as we find forgiveness from God for our own sins. While the curse of sin that resulted from the Fall may give the impression that having a good marriage is impossible, we know that when God is the center of our relationship, our marriages will be blessed beyond any expectation.

Singleness

"But I say to the unmarried and to the widows: It is good for them if they remain even as I am; but if they cannot exercise self-control, let them marry." (1 Corinthians 7:8-9a)

How can being single play a positive role in our relationship with God and others? Doesn't singleness imply an inability to either establish a relationship or maintain one? Those who are single are often feared as a possible threat to other people's marriages, pitied for their inability to "snag someone," or considered self-centered because they aren't taking care of a husband and children. Yet none of these may be true of a single, and usually are not. Singles, even more than those who are married, have greater opportunity to serve God and minister to others:

"He who is unmarried cares for the things of the Lord—how he may please the Lord. But he who is married cares about the things of the world—how he may please his wife. There is a difference between a wife and a virgin. The unmarried woman cares about the things of the Lord, that she may be holy both in body and in spirit. But she who is married cares about the things of the world—how she may please

her husband. And this I say for your own profit, not that I may put a leash on you, but for what is proper, and that you may serve the Lord without distraction." (1 Corinthians 7:32b-25)

Singles have a choice that married people do not: to be wholly devoted to the Lord. Since they do not have the responsibility of being a wife and mother or husband and father, they have more time to give to their relationship with God and others. While this is true, finding other people who are willing to give their time to a relationship can be hard. As a single gets older, most of the people around them will be married. Those who are married will be restricted in the time they can give by family responsibilities, assumptions, or false expectations. Perhaps those who are married think they need to find someone, or think there would be nothing in common to keep a relationship going. Neither is true. Relationships between married couples and singles **are** possible. If we both love God there is always something in common to talk about. But, just like any other relationship, if God is not the source and center of that relationship, there are going to be problems that will eventually cause the relationship to fail.

While singles may be envied for the freedom they have, that freedom can be both a blessing and a curse. Yes, they can spend time on their schedule, doing what they choose; but there may be a great desire for physical intimacy and having children, which is never fulfilled. While it is true that the freedom that singles enjoy lends itself toward self-centeredness, it also provides greater opportunity for service.

One of the ways in which having more time and freedom can be a disadvantage is that there is more opportunity to misspend that time and freedom in sinful ways. When living in a house with other people, or even just one person, we are easily "kept out of trouble" because there are obligations that occupy us and help to keep us from abusing our time. For a single person who desires to be conformed to the image of Christ, determining how to spend free time can be a struggle. Even if some of that time is spent in ministry, there will still be time left over that is difficult to know what to do with.

Living in a culture that exalts having a good time and feeling good, the temptation is to consider whatever time that we are not at work to be time for us; that it is okay to do what we feel like doing, as long as "it doesn't hurt anyone." Our day easily gets divided into time for us, and time spent in labor. As there doesn't seem to be anything wrong with this approach, we settle into a very self-centered life. Because the "me time" is all about the pursuit of pleasure, comfort, and convenience, that is what we end up living for. Our relationship with God gets practically obliterated in the process. As a child of God, there is no such thing as "me time." It is all God's time. We are "bought with a price" (1 Corinthians 6:20). What we have is His. We have a choice: to see our time as belonging to Him, and use it for His glory, in obedience and ministry, or to use it for ourselves.

Singles can be busy in ministry and give the appearance of devoted service, but what they serve may very well be the hope of getting married. It is a natural desire to be married; but like all natural desires, it can become what we live for. Why is this? Why is marriage sought after so diligently? There are two common reasons: the fear of growing old alone and seeing marriage as a solution to loneliness. But does marriage provide completeness? In answering this we must ask another question: Who created us? (Genesis 1-3). We will only ever find our completion in God, not in any institution He provided for us. Do we marry so we won't be lonely? No. If it is God who completes us, no man or woman can prevent us from feeling lonely.

Loneliness is a feeling of isolation and a desire for comfort, connection, or companionship. Most of all, it is not being understood or not feeling loved or accepted. I cannot help but think of the hymn "No One Understands Like Jesus." This song emphasizes a very important point: that no one can compare with the Lord Jesus Christ in comfort, love, consolation, and understanding.

This does not mean that there aren't moments of connectedness with others; but whatever we will experience from another person cannot compare in quality or consistency with what God provides. Other believers can be good friends or good marriage partners, but they will fail us, whether it is intentional or not. We will fail each other because we all see and experience things from our own perspective. Our perspective is based on personality, temperament, spiritual state, and past and present experiences (including what we have been taught). The combination for each person is going to be unique; though we can relate, we will not experience the same event in the same way. We can have sympathy and compassion, but we cannot know exactly what someone else is experiencing or has experienced. Only God, who has created us and knows us better than we know ourselves, can do this. As believers, children of God, we can never truly say that we are alone, for Jesus has promised never to leave or forsake us (Hebrews 13:5). If we are alone or feel lonely, He has not left us.

Anytime we choose to sin, that sin will separate us from God: "If I regard wickedness in my heart, the Lord will not hear" (Psalm 66:18). But when loneliness comes as a result of testing or trial, we need to remember that any abandonment that is felt is only a feeling. Even if we cannot feel God or see Him doing anything, Jesus has promised not to abandon us — and He does not break His promises.

Loneliness is a state or condition brought about not by separation from people, but from God. This is why loneliness is not limited to those who are single; many married people acknowledge being lonely. It may not be a lack of physical or emotional connection with another person, but a lack of fellowship with God. So what do we do when we are feeling lonely? Instead of looking to a marriage partner to take away our loneliness, look to God and repent of anything blocking fellowship with Him. When we do spend time focusing on God, centered on Him, we find that God is the best companion and friend we can have.

If we really, really want to get married and we do not surrender this desire to the Lord, our future marriage partner will become what we serve, not God. When we live for the possibility of getting married, all that we say and do is done with this in mind. This results in viewing people (especially single Christians) only in the light of how they support or fulfill our hope of marriage. It also means living in bondage to that which is temporal and cannot satisfy as God only can; life is filled with anxiety and frustration. To live in this way is destructive; people are not appreciated for who they are, but only for what they do for us. Most importantly, it destroys our relationship with God, for we have ceased living for Him. The bottom line: it prevents us from loving God (and receiving love from Him) and loving others.

Being single truly can be a blessing, if we choose to use the freedom and time we have been given to pursue God. Our challenge is to spend time investing in eternity, rather than living for ourselves. The question we need to ask ourselves is not "what do I want to do?," but "How would God want me to use this time?" or, "What can I do to honor God?"

Being single is not necessarily easier than being married; the trials faced and the circumstances are simply different. Those who are single should not envy those who are married, and vice versa. There are advantages and disadvantages to both; the key for either state is to find contentment in God, not in other people or circumstances.

Church

> *"And He put all things under His feet, and gave Him to be head over all things to the church, which is His body, the fullness of Him who fills all in all." (Ephesians 1:22-23)*

What is the purpose of church? Instructions are given in Scripture as to order in the church service, qualifications for elders, pastors, and deacons, as well as the role of spiritual gifts. When Paul was addressing Timothy he admonished him to "Preach the word! Be ready in season and out of season. Convince, rebuke, exhort, with all longsuffering and teaching" (2 Timothy 4:2). Colossians 3:16 tells us to "Let the word of Christ dwell in you richly in all wisdom, teaching and admonishing one another in psalms and hymns and spiritual songs, singing with grace in your hearts to the Lord." The primary purpose of church is worship. I Corinthians 10:31 states: "Therefore, whether you eat or drink, or whatever you do, do all to the glory of God." If what we are doing in the church is not being done to the glory of God, how can any of God's purposes for us be accomplished?

The bottom line is not evangelism, edification, exhortation, or any form of ministry or activity which we commit ourselves to. The bottom line is: "… in whatsoever you do, do all to the glory of God" (1 Corinthians 10:31). The church's mission still remains to evangelize, disciple, encourage and exhort; but to do any of these things for any other purpose than glorifying God is to only accomplish that which will be consumed at the judgment seat of Christ. If whatever we are doing is not flowing out of our relationship with God, it is being done in the flesh. That which motivates us determines whether the action is honoring to God, not just the action itself. If God's Word is accurately taught or preached, but is done with the wrong motive, it does not nullify the effectiveness of God's Word; it does mean that to minister from a wrong motive will not result in blessing. Whether it is teaching a Bible study or washing the dishes, we honor God when He is exalted. To say: "I am going to serve God" or "I am honoring God because I am doing …" is to place the emphasis on ourselves; but to say: "Lord, I need You; only by Your grace and strength can I do Your will. What do You want me to do? Where do You want me to go?" places the emphasis on God.

Why Am I So Miserable If This is the Lord's Will

Worship is attributing worth to someone or something. To worship God is to attribute worth and give glory to Him. In the activities of a church, when honor and glory are given to God in attitude, action, and means, He is glorified. All three are needed to have true worship of God. It does not just "happen." It is a choice each person makes to be humble before the Lord and exalt Him. When worship is not chosen and planned for, what usually happens is that we "go through the motions;" no worship takes place, only the appearance of it. Unless we choose to fix our minds firmly on Christ, God, His Spirit, and His Word, there will be no worship, for we will be distracted by focusing on other things.

When either doctrine or emotional experience is the primary focus, God isn't the focus. While each church should love God's Word, there is a danger that those in teaching and preaching ministries may pick and choose from the Word what they want to emphasize in such a way that it results in hindering the church body's relationship with God and with each other. When what we are teaching and how we are teaching it are of the most importance, church leaders will relate to other believers only in the context of how they support their teaching or preaching ministry. Jesus' message to the church at Ephesus (Revelation 2) commended them for their solid doctrine, but reproved them for losing their first love.

Emotional experiences can also lead us to think that we are focused on God when we are not. If we are focusing on how our worship makes us feel, we are not exalting God. This does not mean that our emotions are not involved when we exalt Him. True worship will create an increased desire to exalt God. But, if we define worship as always having an emotional high, our focus is on ourselves, not on God. True worship puts all of the focus on God and is given without any expectation of something in return. Although nothing is expected, what we will always receive is an increased appreciation and love for God.

Worship results in love for God; love for God compels us to worship. How is this love manifested? How is it recognized? Is it making dinners for the sick? Coming to every service? Saying all the right things? 1 Corinthians 13 defines love for us; the difficulty we have is in understanding how what the Bible describes is carried out. This leads to another question: is love being defined by cultural standards or biblical standards?

When love is defined by cultural standards, certain behaviors are expected, whether or not they truly demonstrate love or not. A cultural standard of love may be seen as things you do for others, while it neglects the development and fostering of relationships. If what we are doing is not an initial step in building relationships with others, love will not have its full expression. God expressed His love for us through the death of His Son, making relationships possible; but His love for us is such that He wants not only to be our Savior, but also our Father. The sacrifice was made so that we would be able to talk to Him, listen to Him, and be comforted, forgiven and healed by Him — that we could know Him.

Both a genuine love and humility will best be evident in how a church prays, and in what it prays for. The Lord gave us His example of prayer in Matthew 6 and Luke 11, in which he illustrated that prayers are to begin with an acknowledgment of God's will and a desire to live according to it. Then comes a demonstration of our dependence on Him to provide that which we need to live, and asking for forgiveness of sin and forgiveness of others' sin against us and help with our struggle with sin and temptation, while expressing confidence in His goodness, power, and strength to accomplish it.

Humility will also be seen in what the leadership and the people of the church put their confidence in. Are strategies, plans, programs, people, or formulas how we depend on things to get accomplished? When we put our confidence in the Lord, we trust Him to get things accomplished in His way and in His timing; as a result, He is glorified.

When a church is not making God the focus, either the Pastor, the music leader/group, or the people attending are the focus. One might protest, "What is the harm of a service that appeals to people?" The harm is that any ministry that is people-centered will only produce self-centered or people-centered Christians, rather than God-centered Christians. The moment that a church starts trying to blend in with the world (instead of not conforming to it, Romans 12:1-2) it is no longer fulfilling its purpose of worship. How is this being done today? Preaching is toned down; there is no more confrontation of sin, only "feel good" sermons. Music is changed: louder, more beat, less doctrine. The emphasis becomes a positive experience for the participant, but at the expense of their benefit and God's glory. We cannot make worldly activities Christian simply by bringing them into church. "That which is born of the flesh is flesh, and that which is born of the Spirit is spirit." (John 3:6); "There can be no darkness where there is light" (1 John 1:5-6).

A church that facilitates God-centered Christians seeks to discover and develop the spiritual gift in each member, and gives them opportunity for service. It will be actively aware of its continual need of God and will not attempt to do anything without dependence, obedience and submission to Him.

Having said this, what if a God-centered church cannot be found? What is a person to do then? Hebrews 10:23-25 gives us the answer:

"Let us hold fast the confession of our hope without wavering, for He who promised is faithful; and let us consider how to stimulate one another to love and good deeds, not forsaking our own assembling together, as is the habit of some, but encouraging one another; and all the more, as you see the day drawing near."

The best way we can encourage one another is to pray, asking for at least one person who has the desire to give glory to God, so that together you can encourage one another to focus on Him. Pray for opportunities for service, doing whatever can be done to bring glory to God. What other people are not doing must not keep us from loving and serving God. Most of all, pray for your church and your church leaders, that they will develop a greater love for God and desire to glorify Him above all else. "Brethren, pray for us!" (1 Thessalonians 5:25)

A church's role is to encourage and exhort its members to seek God themselves, and not to rely solely on what they receive from the pulpit, church service and through others. This does not mean that there is no need for any of these things, only that God is what we need most of all. 1 Peter 2:2 reminds us that we have to make the Word of God part of us in order for us to grow. "As newborn babes, desire the pure milk of the word, that you may grow thereby."

How do we know a church worships God? We can explore the programs and worship, and discover whether the leaders and pastor of a church:

* Strive to be more acceptable to men or to God
* Base standards on God's Word or on popular opinion
* Hold fast to and stand for the truth or water it down a bit
* Emphasize feelings and experience rather than God's Word and focusing on Him

We need to ask if the people:

* Seek to discern the truth? Or, simply believe what they are told?

- Seem satisfied with mediocrity?
- Demonstrate love to one another?
- Seek to pursue God above all else?

A church fails to accomplish its purpose when it does not:

- Teach or preach the "whole counsel of God"
- Provide a place of worship (where communion and baptism by water is practiced)
- Provide opportunities for service appropriate to the spiritual gifts of its members
- Provide a place for edification, exhortation, confrontation of sin, and encouragement of the believers
- Seek to evangelize the lost and support missions

When selecting a church, the criteria should not include what it does for us; meaning, does it provide friendship, social activities, etc. that we want? When we aim to find a church for the purpose of meeting our own needs, we will end up going from church to church, never quite happy or satisfied with what we find. One thing about a church is liked, but not another; so we move on, and end up never joining and committing ourselves to a local congregation of believers.

Seeking a church while not being concerned about what it does for us may seem like the pursuit of a loveless God, but it is not. When we take our eyes off of ourselves and focus them on God by worshiping Him, loving Him, thanking and praising Him, thinking and meditating on all that He is and has done, we find that He meets our needs far better, exceedingly beyond any attempt that we make to meet them on our own. We are created to glorify God; when we pursue any other purpose or goal, we never achieve what we want and will always come up short and leave dissatisfied.

A church cannot meet our deepest needs; neither can people. We are all sinners saved by grace; put another way, we are all broken, flawed people. We can always find something wrong in a church if we look for it, for it is full of sinners. The only One who is and was without sin is Jesus Christ; it is only He who completes us and will never fail us. God may use a church or people at times to be the conduit by which He ministers to us. But our dependence is never to be on a church or people; rather, it is always to be on God. He is what we need most of all.

Why Am I So Miserable If This is the Lord's Will

"…to deny ourselves means to bar ourselves from … being influenced by these negative feelings. Interestingly, the definition 'barring ourselves from following something' comes from the Greek root meaning of the word to suffer. When we bar ourselves from doing what we want, what we feel and what we desire, we often do suffer." [22]

"Lament and mourn and weep! Let your laughter be turned to mourning and your joy to gloom."

– *James 4:9*

"Do not rejoice over me, my enemy; When I fall, I will arise; when I sit in darkness, the LORD will be a light to me. I will bear the indignation of the LORD, because I have sinned against Him, until He pleads my case and executes justice for me. He will bring me forth to the light; I will see His righteousness."

– *Micah 7:8-9*

Chapter 7
Defeating the Flesh

*A*n analogy from Scripture which illustrates the victorious Christian life is given in Hebrews 12: 1-2:

> *"Therefore we also, since we are surrounded by so great a cloud of witnesses, let us lay aside every weight, and the sin which so easily entangles us, and let us run with endurance the race that is set before us, looking unto Jesus, the author and finisher of our faith, who for the joy that was set before Him endured the cross, despising the shame, and has sat down at the right hand of the throne of God."*

In this passage is not only what we need to do to live victoriously, but also why and how to do it. We are to: 1) lay aside every weight and sin; and 2) run with endurance. How? By looking unto Jesus. Why? 1) For the same joy Jesus endured the cross for; and 2) to live the same victorious life that all the men and women of faith (as recorded in Hebrews 11), have lived.

Just as a runner cannot win the race if he carries extra weight, we cannot live a victorious Christian life if we are weighed down. What weighs us down is anything that prevents us from yielding to, depending on, or following Jesus Christ. This can be anything that violates God's commands (sin), or any other activity. How do we get weighed down? It all comes down to the choices we make every day. Do we choose activities that glorify God, and don't take our eyes off of Him? While all children of God desire to glorify Him, we often end up making a choice that serves us, not Him. To make the choice to serve Him will always require self-denial or self-sacrifice. Sacrifice as a choice we make is recorded in Romans 12:1, 2:

> *"I beseech you therefore, brethren, by the mercies of God, that you present your bodies a living sacrifice, holy, acceptable to God, which is your reasonable service. And do not be conformed to this world, but be transformed by the renewing of your mind, that you may prove what is that good and acceptable and perfect will of God."*

This passage further explains how we sacrifice our lives to Him: by the mercies of God. We cannot live the Christian life in our own strength, but must utterly depend on God for the grace and mercy we need to make God-honoring choices. We also see in this passage that not living like the world or according to fleshly desires will require the choice to renew our mind in the truth of God's Word.

Self-denial as a choice we make is recorded in Matthew 16: 24: "Then Jesus said to His disciples, 'If anyone desires to come after Me, let him deny himself, and take up his cross, and follow Me.'" As a cross meant crucifixion and death, self-denial is self-sacrifice: laying all that you have and are at Jesus' feet.

Just as Jesus suffered on the cross for us, we are to expect that following Him requires us to deny our fleshly desires, to suffer in the flesh. 1 Peter 4:1-2 tells us that "Therefore, since Christ has suffered in the flesh, arm yourselves also with the same purpose, because he who has suffered in the flesh has ceased from sin, so as to live the rest of time in the flesh no longer for the lusts of men, but for the will of God." The suffering mentioned here is not the suffering we endure for the cause of Christ, as when we are persecuted for being a Christian, or for teaching about Jesus Christ. This type of suffering is described in Romans 8:35: "… tribulation, or distress, or persecution, or famine, or nakedness, or peril, or sword." The suffering mentioned here is simply the same kind of suffering that a runner will experience as he prepares for and runs a race. A runner may experience muscle strain, bruises, broken bones, and various other aches and pains. Yet none of these things keep him from running. He runs despite all this because of the joy and exhilaration he receives.

The choice that Peter calls for is the choice to set our minds toward the goal of living in and for the will of God, and not to live in the flesh for the lusts of men. To deny the flesh what it wants doesn't mean it won't be painful. But Peter reminds us that Jesus also suffered in the flesh for us; suffering in the flesh is something that should not be dismissed.

It may be difficult to grasp this concept. It is one thing to accept suffering that comes our way, but to accept the suffering that comes with obedience? God does want us to put the deeds of the flesh to death (Romans 8:13), which means suffering. To deny the flesh is to cause it to suffer; to deny the flesh and walk in the Spirit (doing the will of God) is to experience the fruit of the Spirit.

"The Spirit Himself bears witness with our spirit that we are children of God, and if children, then heirs—heirs of God and joint heirs with Christ, if indeed we suffer with Him, that we may also be glorified together. For I consider that the sufferings of this present time are not worthy to be compared with the glory which shall be revealed in us." (Romans 8:16-18)

That God would ask us to endure suffering or that He would even allow it is unthinkable in this day and age. This is a result of a misunderstanding of the love of God, that it is His desire to know Him more intimately and be conformed to the image of His Son. This cannot be accomplished unless we are willing to yield to His will and deny ourselves. **Any suffering we go through cannot even remotely compare to the joy that is found in knowing Him and in doing His will.**

We need to expect spiritual conflict. Remember what Paul tells us in Galatians 5:17: "the flesh lusts against the Spirit and the Spirit against the flesh; and these are contrary to one another, so that you do not do the things that you wish." If the flesh is denied what it desires, it will feel like suffering. The flesh always lies to us that we cannot live without _____. But this is not true. We will suffer if we give it up—but we will also know the joy of obedience.

Suffering, as long as we live on this earth, is unavoidable. There is suffering for doing what is right (walking in the Spirit, living in obedience to God's Word; or, for being a Christian and testifying of Him), and there is suffering for doing what is wrong (walking according to the flesh, and not obeying God). There is suffering that comes about as a result of circumstances beyond our control. But there, too, we have a choice; we can choose how, by God's grace, we are going to respond to it.

I thank God for His grace and help during our time of need! Whether it is the suffering we chose to experience in dying to the flesh and turning from sin or the suffering we experience due to trial, circumstance, or for our faith, our God is faithful and by His grace we are able to stand. "Watch, stand fast in the faith, be brave, be strong" (1 Corinthians 16:13).

Misery's Solution

But what if we are accepting the suffering in our lives, yet we are miserable? Misery says: "I see that what I do and say does not work; I fail at my relationships, at work, at life." "I see the damage I have done to my life and the life of others; I cannot be anything other than what I am, so what is the use?" "This is hopeless." "I have tried to do what is right, but I fail continually. What God asks is impossible!" These are all lies of our enemy, Satan.

In the first chapter of this book, I described how I became miserable because I was trying to live the Christian life in my own strength. I had thought that since I was in God's will that I should be blessed for obeying His Word. I did not expect miserable circumstances! While I wanted to do God's will, I was still miserable; I had accepted the circumstances in my life, but I felt a sense of futility and hopelessness. I sought to alleviate my misery by doing anything that might make me feel better. I treated myself with food, watched TV or read novels to try to alleviate my emotional pain. I did whatever was socially and culturally acceptable that did not overtly break any of God's laws. This did not work and will never work, for seeking any fleshly solution is in opposition to God. It also did not work because the flesh provides only a temporary fix, and it left me more miserable than before. The crazy part of it is that even if a fleshly solution only made it worse, I continued on that path for a while because I felt that some relief was better than none. This, too, is a lie.

Doing things my way didn't fill the void I felt. It did not soothe my conscience and I had no peace; in the end, my misery was worse than it was before. Life really did seem pointless and meaningless.

If life seems futile, that's because it is — **without** the purpose and meaning that God gives to it and the ability He gives us to accomplish anything of worth and value. If we are miserable in our suffering, it is because our eyes have become focused on our circumstances rather than on God. This explains why we can be in the will of God and be miserable. If we are where we should be, doing what we should be doing, yet are not focused on, submitted to, or resting on God, we will be miserable. Rather than just stoically accepting our lot in life, we can have peace, joy, and contentment in the worst circumstances when we see everything in light of whom and what God is. We can rejoice and be thankful because we know He loves us; He will sustain us and cause all things to work out for good in our lives. Life only becomes hopeless when our hope is not in God. "Now hope does not disappoint, because the love of God has been poured out in our hearts by the Holy Spirit who was given to us." (Romans 5:5)

What is the solution to misery, boredom, loneliness, stress, or pain? How do we address our emotional needs? Prayer requests given at church more often than not are for physical or circumstantial needs; but do we really trust the Lord to take care of our emotional needs?

A song that I learned as a child really irked me. It began: "Happiness is, to know the Savior...." I really did not like that song, for I was not a happy child. I thought, "Yeah, right." I loved the Lord; I had depended on Him as I encountered difficult circumstances. Despite this, I was not happy, and blamed my unhappiness on the people and circumstances I was stuck with. Like many people, happiness became a thing only encountered for brief moments of time, when either I got something I wanted or something enjoyable happened. I did not know how to enjoy life or be happy unless it was on my terms.

I knew that happiness is a choice and that if I depended on circumstances for it, I would be lost. But in spite of this, I kept going back to things I knew made me feel good. I tried doing this, but whatever emotional funk I was in at the time would not magically go away. I watched and observed other Christians and saw how they, too, looked to events/activities, circumstances, or people for their happiness, and I thought that perhaps this was normal, and

I should just continue to find happiness where I could (as long as it didn't violate Scripture or hurt anyone).The only problem is that when happiness is pursued in this way, it never is truly obtained and has to be continually pursued. Instead of really being able to enjoy life, most of life becomes what we muck through to get to the stuff we really enjoy. What a miserable way to live!

What is the answer then? The answer is two-fold. The first part is both the key to happiness and the means: knowing God, our Savior, and the Spirit. As much as I am loath to admit it, the song I learned as I child is right: happiness is to know the Savior. But knowing the Savior needs to be more than just head knowledge, or even a remembrance of past experiences. It is the knowledge spoken of in Philippians 3:10a, "that I may know Him...". "Know" here is ginōksō: to know by observation and experience.[23] Happiness is seeking to experience God on a continual basis; it is looking to Him for the solution to whatever emotional difficulty is being experienced, whether it is boredom or pain. When this happens, our happiness is found in Him, not in our circumstances. There is nothing or no one who can "make" us happy; only knowing God brings real happiness and makes enjoying everything else possible.

The second part is a command from Scripture: "Rejoice in the Lord always; again I say rejoice!" (Philippians 4:4) Notice that the command is repeated twice! Psalm 118:24 also commands: "This is the day that the LORD has made; let us rejoice and be glad in it." In the book of Psalms alone, rejoicing in the Lord is mentioned at least 45 times. Rejoicing in the Lord is more than just thanking Him for our salvation; it is reveling in all He is. I mentioned Psalm 118:24 especially because it illustrates that our ability to live life with joy is because of the surety we have in God. We can rejoice in **this** day, no matter what this day brings, because we know all things are in His mighty loving hands; that nothing lives, breathes, exists apart from His making it happen. This second part is only possible if the first part is true;

trying to put it into practice without knowing and loving God will only be another work of the flesh.

When we are wiped out physically, emotionally, or mentally, rejoicing in the Lord may seem impossible. Rejoicing in the Lord does not mean plastering a smile on our face while we are suffering on the inside. It is declaring to ourselves the God that we have, and claiming what He is for our situation. When we are exhausted, God is our strength and He will enable us to do what we need to do. Rejoicing in the Lord is declaring: "You are my strength!" "You are my help in time of need!" We can rejoice because even if people or circumstances let us down or hurt us, and we don't know why things are the way they are, we **do know** our God! Our God **is** good! He is kind, loving, holy, true, and faithful; He is our provider, our healer, our comforter and our Savior!

Though we usually interpret feeling miserable as being neglected or abandoned by God, God is never more clearly known than when we suffer. When all that the flesh and this world offer fails us, God is **always** faithful. It is in time of trial, loss, and pain that the preciousness of our Savior is more clearly revealed to us. This is why the Apostle Paul declared in Philippians 3:8, 10 that he considered "...all things loss in view of the surpassing value of knowing Christ Jesus my Lord, for whom I have suffered the loss of all things, and count them as rubbish in order that I may gain Christ...that I may know Him, and the power of His resurrection and the fellowship of His sufferings, being conformed to His death..."

Notice that knowing God, knowing Christ, is intertwined with suffering! To gain Christ—and thereby gain real happiness—we need to suffer the loss of what the flesh considers pleasurable and necessary to enjoy life. We cannot find happiness, joy, peace, contentment, satisfaction, healing, strength, or comfort unless we turn away from all that appeals to our flesh and pursue God. This may not make sense to us when we are being tested; but it is in time of temptation and trial that we are given opportunity to put our faith and trust in God. If all that misery does is help us see how inadequate we are at achieving any kind of peace, joy, contentment and satisfaction apart from God, it is well worth it. Have we gotten so caught up in enjoying what He has given that we have forgotten that the Giver is so much greater than any of His gifts? There is always cause for rejoicing in God!

We know that God is good; will we trust Him or trust what our feelings are telling us? Will we choose to rejoice that God is for us and not believe what the flesh keeps promising (and not delivering!)? God will not ever fail; our feelings will. When we choose to rejoice in all God is, we trust Him to "work all things together for good to those that love God and are called according to His purpose" (Romans 8:28)—even if it does not feel good at the time! It is only through rejoicing in the LORD of hosts that any true, meaningful happiness is found; rejoicing in anything else is to focus on and depend on that which will fail us and lead to misery, not happiness.

Once we run to God for deliverance, and gladly surrender our will, embracing His, comes the realization that what we thought was bondage (doing His will, not being able to please the flesh) is actually immense, complete freedom like we have never experienced before. We do not have to stay on the treadmill of the flesh! When we choose to serve God, rather than self, we find that God is so much better: greater, kinder, more loving, gracious, and faithful than we could ever be to ourselves. Also, when we love God, we aren't ever **forced** to do His will. We **want** to do His will. The only time our behavior is forced or compelled is when we let other people manipulate us or when we try to do what is right out of a sense of duty rather than love. Yes, when we submit to God, He is our King. He is our Master. But what a wonderful, loving Master we have! There is no better Master than He.

Will we be a slave to ourselves, our flesh, or a slave to God? Will we let how we feel dictate our actions and life? Or will we rely on God to supply our needs and not the flesh? We cannot love God, serve Him and be obsessed with our fleshly desires. Rather the opposite: we are, as the Apostle Paul says, to put off the flesh: "That you put off, concerning your former conduct, the old man which grows corrupt according to the deceitful lusts" (Ephesians 4:22). Whatever fleshly characteristics or desires we have are to be considered a dirty, worn-out garment to be thrown out. The flesh cannot be killed, but we can choose to die to it and walk in the Spirit.

Are You Miserable? Depressed? Then:

* Rejoice! If we have Christ, then no matter what the circumstance, we have something to rejoice in. "Rejoice in the Lord always. Again I will say, rejoice!" (Philippians 4:4) What is the worst thing that can happen to you? The worst thing would be to lose your salvation, which won't ever happen. Any pain that is experienced here on earth is temporary, and God will always give us the grace we need when we need it. "Seeing then that we have a great High Priest who has passed through the heavens, Jesus the Son of God, let us hold fast our confession. For we do not have a High Priest who cannot sympathize with our weaknesses, but was in all points tempted as we are, yet without sin" (Hebrews 4:14-15).

* Stop living for what might happen and start living for God now. "For me to live is Christ, to die is gain" (Philippians 1:21). How can life, people, or God be enjoyed now, if all of our energies are being invested in a preferred future?

* Praise God for the unique personality, gifts, abilities, or physical characteristics He has given each of us. "I will praise you for I am fearfully and wonderfully made; marvelous are thy works, and that my soul knows very well" (Psalm 139:14). God does not ever make mistakes! God has allowed or given what He has for a reason. Based

Why Am I So Miserable If This is the Lord's Will

on what He has promised in His Word, and on His character, we know it is for our good.

- Trust what God does and allows, knowing that He cannot do wrong or evil, and loves us perfectly. "Trust in the LORD with all your heart, and lean not on your own understanding" (Proverbs 3:5). Do we really believe that He is withholding something from us that we need, or that He is being "unfair" in what He is giving or allowing?

- Choose what and in whom you will believe. "For this reason I also suffer these things; nevertheless I am not ashamed, for I know whom I have believed and am persuaded that He is able to keep what I have committed to Him until that day" (2 Timothy 1:12). Has God ever been unfaithful, untrustworthy, or untrue? Considering the alternatives, why would we choose to believe in anything or anyone else? (Do we think we can do better, or that anyone else could?)

- Be humble before the Lord (James 4:10). To attempt to live the Christian life in our own strength, by our own means is not humility. Humility recognizes that "I can do all things through Christ who strengthens me" (Philippians 4:13). To say this in the negative: "I cannot do anything, or accomplish anything without Christ strengthening me."

What do all these actions have in common? They each result in putting our focus on God and taking it off of ourselves and our circumstances. Misery's solution is always to keep our minds focused on God. "You will keep him in perfect peace, whose mind is stayed on You, because he trusts in You" (Isaiah 26:3).

While there is suffering that results from the loss of what the flesh desires, may we never experience the suffering that comes as a result of our own sin and leads to misery! Suffering, as long as we are on this earth, is unavoidable

—the question is, are we going to suffer for choosing what is right or for choosing evil?

STOP trying to make this life work on your terms—it is a hopeless cause that only ends in misery.

LIVE for the better hope and joy of knowing God, loving God and serving Him.

"Why are you cast down, O my soul? And why are you disquieted within me? Hope in God, for I shall yet praise Him" (Psalm 42:5).

End Notes

1. Partow, Donna. This Isn't the Life I Signed Up for. Minneapolis, Mn.: Bethany House, c2003.

2. Piper, John, Future Grace. Colorado Springs, Co.: Multnomah Publishers, 1995.

3. Bennett, Arthur G., ed., Valley of Vision. Carlisle, Pa: Banner of Truth, 2003.

4. Sanders, J. Oswald. In Pursuit of Maturity. Grand Rapids, Mi.: Lamplighter books, c1986.

5. Julian, Ron, Righteous Sinners: The Believer's Struggle with Faith, Grace, and Works. Colorado Springs, Co. : NavPress, c1998.

6. Julian, Ron, Righteous Sinners: The Believer's Struggle with Faith, Grace, and Works. Colorado Springs, Co. : NavPress, c1998

7. Bennett, Arthur G., ed., Valley of Vision. Carlisle, Pa: Banner of Truth, 2003.

8. Strong's Dictionary of the Greek Testament

9. MacArthur, John F. Jr., The Vanishing Conscience. Thomas Nelson, 2005.

10. Lutzer, Erwin, Managing Your Emotions. Victor Books, 1983.

11. Bennett, Arthur G , ed., Valley of Vision. Carlisle, Pa: Banner of Truth, 2003.

12. Crabb, Larry. The Pressure's Off. Waterbrook Press, 2002.

13. Burroughs, Jeremiah. The Evil of Evils. Soli Deo Gloria publications, 1992

14. Crabb, Larry, Shattered Dreams: God's unexpected path to joy. Waterbrook Press, 2002.

15. Piper, John, Future Grace. Colorado Springs, Co.: Multnomah Publishers, 1995.

16. Simpson, A. B. Christ in you. Camp Hill, Pa.: Christian publications, c1997.

17. Bennet, Arthur G., ed., Valley of Vision. Carlisle, Pa: Banner of Truth, 2003.

18. Piper, John, Future Grace. Colorado Springs, Co.: Multnomah Publishers, 1995.

19. Neufeldt, Victoria, and Guralink, David B., editors. Webster's New World Dictionary. Third College edition. New York: Webster's New World Dictionaries, 1989.

20. Missler, Chuck and Missler, Nancy. The Way of Agape. Coeur d'Adlene, ID: King's High Way Ministries, c1994.

21. Bunyon, John. The Pilgrim's Progress From This World To That Which Is To Come. New York: Heritage Press, 1942.

22. Missler, Chuck and Missler, Nancy. The Way Of Agape. Coeur d'Adlene, ID: King's High Way Ministries, c1994.

23. Strong, James, ed., The New Strong's Expanded Dictionary Of Bible Words. Nashville, TN : Thomas Nelson Publishers, c2001.